前言 *PREFACE*

英国思想家培根说过：阅读使人深刻。阅读的真正目的是获取信息，开拓视野和陶冶情操。从语言学习的角度来说，学习语言若没有大量阅读就如隔靴搔痒，因为阅读中的语言是最丰富、最灵活、最具表现力、最符合生活情景的，同时读物中的情节、故事引人入胜，进而能充分调动读者的阅读兴趣，培养读者的文学修养，至此，语言的学习水到渠成。

"麦格希中英双语阅读文库"在世界范围内选材，涉及科普、社会文化、文学名著、传奇故事、成长励志等多个系列，充分满足英语学习者课外阅读之所需，在阅读中学习英语、提高能力。

◎难度适中

本套图书充分照顾读者的英语学习阶段和水平，从读者的阅读兴趣出发，以难易适中的英语语言为立足点，选材精心、编排合理。

◎精品荟萃

本套图书注重经典阅读与实用阅读并举。既包含国内外脍炙人口、耳熟能详的美文，又包含科普、人文、故事、励志类等多学科的精彩文章。

◎功能实用

本套图书充分体现了双语阅读的功能和优势，充分考虑到读者课外阅读的方便，超出核心词表的词汇均出现在使其意义明显的语境之中，并标注释义。

鉴于编者水平有限，凡不周之处，谬误之处，皆欢迎批评教正。

我们真心地希望本套图书承载的文化知识和英语阅读的策略对提高读者的英语著作欣赏水平和英语运用能力有所裨益。

丛书编委会

社会文化系列

麦格希 中英双语阅读文库

亚当·斯密的《国富论》

世界新知馆 第1辑

麦格希中英双语阅读文库编委会 ● 编

吉林出版集团股份有限公司

图书在版编目（CIP）数据

世界新知馆.第1辑,亚当·斯密的《国富论》/美
国麦格劳-希尔教育集团主编;麦格希中英双语阅读文库
编委会编;张威,孟令坤译. -- 2版. -- 长春:吉林
出版集团股份有限公司,2018.3
（麦格希中英双语阅读文库）
书名原文:Timed Readings Plus in Social Studies Book 6
ISBN 978-7-5581-4794-4

Ⅰ.①世… Ⅱ.①美… ②麦… ③张… ④孟… Ⅲ.
①英语—汉语—对照读物②社会科学—通俗读物 Ⅳ.
①H319.4：C

中国版本图书馆CIP数据核字(2018)第046554号

世界新知馆 第1辑 亚当·斯密的《国富论》

编：麦格希中英双语阅读文库编委会
插 画：齐 航 李延霞
责任编辑：朱 玲 孙琳琳
封面设计：冯冯翼
开 本：660mm×960mm 1/16
字 数：225千字
印 张：10
版 次：2018年3月第2版
印 次：2018年3月第1次印刷

出 版：吉林出版集团股份有限公司
发 行：吉林出版集团外语教育有限公司
地 址：长春市泰来街1825号
邮编：130011
电 话：总编办：0431-86012683
发行部：0431-86012767 0431-86012826(Fax)
印 刷：香河利华文化发展有限公司

ISBN 978-7-5581-4794-4 定价：29.90元

Contents

1

Adam Smith's *Wealth of Nations*

In the history of the United States, the signing of the *Declaration of Independence* is largely thought to be the most *noteworthy* event of 1776. Another *pivotal* advance in thinking, however, took place that same year. *An Inquiry into the Nature and Causes of the Wealth of Nations* was published. Its author, a Scottish

亚当·斯密的《国富论》

在美国历史中，《独立宣言》的签订在很大程度上被认为是1776年最值得注意的一次事件。然而，另外一个在思想上有进步的关键事件也发生在同一年。这就是《国民财富的性质和成因研究》的出版。这本书的作者是一位苏格兰的哲学家，名字叫亚当·斯密。他以现代经济学理论的奠基人而著称。他是第一位概述社会生活、政治、经济有联

---

noteworthy *adj.* 值得注意的；显著的   pivotal *adj.* 关键的

philosopher named Adam Smith, is credited as the founder of modern economic theory. Smith was the first thinker to *outline* the links between social life, politics, and economics.

The book's most enduring concept is the idea of the "*invisible* hand". Smith made a strong case against government control of the economy. He argued that economic systems form and flourish as a natural result of people's activities. People need to make money, so they work to produce goods that others are willing to buy. Sellers, in turn, use the money they earn to buy goods that they need and want. This pattern of producing, buying, and selling creates a *harmonious* social system that requires no outside interference by government. It arises naturally—guided, according to Smith, "as if by an invisible hand." Smith's system, now often called free enterprise, forms the basis of modern capitalism as it is known in the United States today.

系的思想家 。

　　这本书最主要阐述的一个持久的理念是"看不见的手"。斯密在反对政府控制经济上用了一套强有力的论据。他认为经济体系的形成和发展是人类活动的一个自然结果。人们需要挣钱，所以他们工作来生产一些别人愿意买的商品。反过来，卖家用他们的钱去买他们需要和想要的商品。这种生产、买卖和销售的一体模式创立了一个和谐的社会体系，这个体系需要政府不从外在进行干扰。根据斯密的看法，这个体系应该很自然地由"看不见的手"所引导。斯密的体系现在通常被称为自由企业，它奠定了美国资本主义的基础，在今天的美国仍然家喻户晓。

---

philosopher *n.* 哲学家　　　　　　　　outline *v.* 概述；提出……的纲要
invisible *adj.* 看不见的　　　　　　　harmonious *adj.* 和谐的

2

States of the Middle Atlantic Region

The United States is made up of 50 states divided into five *distinct* regions. Located on the East Coast, the Middle Atlantic region was one of the earliest to be *colonized*. European explorers settled in the areas that are the present-day states of New York, New Jersey, Pennsylvania, Delaware, and

大西洋中部地区的各州

美国是由50个州组成，分在5个不同的地区，大西洋中部地区位于东海岸线上，是最早的殖民地之一。欧洲探险家定居在如今的纽约、新泽西、宾夕法尼亚、特拉华和马里兰地区。这些州有很多共同

distinct *adj.* 明显不同的   colonize *v.* 使······殖民地化

Maryland. These states have much in common. Each was among the original 13 states that fought for *independence* and *ratified* the U.S. *Constitution*.

Although the Dutch were the first to settle there, Pennsylvania takes its name from William Penn, who founded it in 1681. Penn, an English Quaker, sought to establish a colony to promote freedom and equality. The colony became a *commonwealth* in 1776. Its largest city, Philadelphia, was the country's first capital. Many momentous events took place there during the Revolution. Among them were the signing of the *Declaration of Independence* and the drafting and signing of the *Constitution*.

In 1664 Dutch merchants started the Dutch West India Company

点。它们都属于原始的13个州，曾经为独立而战，并且通过了美国宪法。

虽然荷兰人是最先到那里定居的，但宾夕法尼亚采用了威廉·佩恩的名字命名，他于1681年建立了该殖民地。佩恩是一名英国贵格会教徒，他力图建立一个促进自由和平等的殖民地。1776年这个殖民地成为联邦，其最大城市费城，是这个国家第一个首都。在革命期间，有很多重大事件都在那儿发生。这些事件中就有《独立宣言》的签署和《宪法》的起草和签署。

1664年荷兰商人沿哈德森河开办了荷兰西印度公司驻地，这些驻地

---

independence *n.* 独立   ratify *v.* 正式批准
constitution *n.* 宪法   commonwealth *n.* 联邦

with posts along the Hudson River. These posts grew into New Netherland. New Netherland had a *thriving* river trade and an excellent harbor. New Jersey was *initially* part of the colony of New Netherland. First colonized by Dutch and Swedish settlers, the state is named for the Isle of Jersey, of which Sir George Carteret, one of its *original* owners, was governor. The state made many important *contributions* to the American Revolution. However, it is perhaps best remembered for Washington's crossing of the Delaware River to fight the British at the Battle of Trenton.

New York, also part of New Netherland, was settled by the Dutch in 1624 but was seized by England in 1664 and renamed for the

---

发展成新尼德兰。新尼德兰曾有过繁荣的河上贸易和优良的港口。新泽西最初是新尼德兰殖民地的一部分。这个州最初被荷兰和瑞典殖民者开拓为殖民地，被命名为泽西岛，乔治·卡特里特先生是统治者，他是这个岛原来的拥有者之一。新泽西为美国革命做出了巨大贡献。然而人们印象最深刻的也许是特伦顿战役中华盛顿穿过特拉华河对抗英国的情景。

纽约也是新尼德兰的一部分，1624年荷兰人在此定居，但1664年被英国占领，并以约克公爵的名字重新命名。在革命期间英国人建立了纽约

---

thriving *adj.* 繁荣的   initially *adv.* 最初地
original *adj.* 起初的   contribution *n.* 贡献

Duke of York. Throughout the Revolution, the British held New York City. New York State was the site of *fierce* battles. New York City—for a short time—served as the capital of the new nation.

The English explorer Henry Hudson discovered Delaware in 1609, but Swedish, Finnish, and Dutch colonists settled it. It was first a Dutch colony; but it was seized by the English in 1664, *recaptured* by the Dutch, and then returned to the English.

Charles I of England chartered Maryland in 1632. It was named for his queen *consort*, Henrietta Maria. Cecilius Calvert, second Baron Baltimore, established the colony as a haven for those fleeing religious *persecution*. Annapolis was the site of the Treaty of Paris, which ended the Revolutionary War.

市。纽约州是激烈战争的遗址。纽约市曾有一段时间是这个新生国家的首都。

1609年英国探险家亨利·哈德森发现特拉华，但是瑞典、芬兰、荷兰殖民者在此殖民。特拉华最初是荷兰的一块殖民地，但1664年英国人占领了它，之后又被荷兰夺回，再后来又重新回到英国。

在1632年，英国国王查理一世特许命名特拉华为马里兰。这是以他皇后的名字亨丽埃塔·玛丽亚命名的。巴尔的摩男爵二世塞西里尤斯·卡尔弗特建立了这个殖民地，把它作为逃离宗教迫害的那些人的避难所。安纳波利斯是签署《巴黎条约》的地方，这个条约的签署标志着革命战争的结束。

---

fierce *adj.* 激烈的　　　　　　　　recapture *v.* 夺回

consort *n.* （尤指统治者的）配偶　　persecution *n.* 迫害

3

William Penn's Legacy

William Penn contributed much to the early history of the United States. Although he may be best known as the founder of Pennsylvania, Penn's *influence* also *extended* to the other states of the Middle Atlantic region.

As a Quaker in England, Penn was jailed for his beliefs. He thought that the

威廉·佩恩的遗产

威廉·佩恩对美国早期历史贡献颇多。虽然他为大众所知可能源于他是宾夕法尼亚的创建者，但他的影响也延伸到了大西洋中部地区的其他各州。

在英国佩恩是一个贵格会教徒，他曾因为自己的信仰而入狱。他认

influence *n.* 影响

extend *v.* 延伸

American colonies offered a chance for equal rights and religious freedom. He wanted to start *settlements* there as a "holy experiment". In 1681 Penn and some others *purchased* East Jersey. He later received a charter for Pennsylvania. He was also granted land, first *annexed* to New York, that would later become the state of Delaware.

Many people considered the *Frame of Government of Pennsylvania*, Penn's plan for the colony, a *document* that was ahead of its time. One of the country's founders, Thomas Jefferson, called Penn "the greatest law-giver the world has produced." Penn was also responsible for planning and naming the city of Philadelphia, which means "the city of brotherly love." In the early days of the colony, he established good relations with the Native Americans

---

为美洲的殖民地提供了一个权利平等和宗教信仰自由的机会。他想要在那里定居，并认为那是"神圣的尝试"。在1681年，佩恩和其他一些人购买了东泽西。之后他得到了英国的特许，建立宾夕法尼亚。他也被授予土地，这土地起初并入纽约，之后就成为了特拉华州。

很多人认为，佩恩为殖民地规划写的《宾夕法尼亚的政府结构》这一文件，是超前于他们所处的时代的。美国的创建者之一托马斯·杰弗逊，称佩恩是"世界创造的最伟大的法律制定者"。佩恩也负责设计和命名费城，它意味着"兄弟之爱的城"。在殖民早期，他与当地的印第安人建立

---

settlement *n.* 定居

annex *v.* 并吞

purchase *v.* 购买

document *n.* 文件

of the area. This helped pave the way for the future growth of the colonies.

In addition to his writings on government, Penn wrote *expansively* on religion and other issues. Today his writings can be found in libraries throughout the country.

了良好的关系。这也为将来殖民地的发展铺平了道路。

他除了在政府方面进行写作外，也广泛地涉足宗教和其他问题。今天他的作品在美国的图书馆中都能找到。

---

expansively *adv.* 广泛地

4

The Shy Angel

Clara Barton, founder of the American Red Cross, gained worldwide honor for her *dedication* to easing human suffering. Her *tireless* work amid the *filth*, disease, and danger of Civil War battles earned her the *nickname* "Angel of the Battlefield".

害羞的天使

克莱拉·巴顿是美国红十字的创始人，她为人们减少痛苦所做的奉献为她赢得了世界范围的荣誉。她孜孜不倦地工作于污秽、疾病和内战战争的危险之中，这使她赢得了"战场上的天使"的绰号。

---

dedication *n.* 奉献
filth *n.* 污物

tireless *adj.* 不知疲劳的
nickname *n.* 绰号

Barton was born into a liberal, *freethinking* family in 1821. She was much younger than her four brothers and sisters, all of whom happily tutored her in math and reading. As a result, by the time she entered school at the age of three, Barton could read, do simple *arithmetic*, and spell three-syllable words. She easily kept up with the older children *academically* but did not fit in with them socially.

Concerned about their daughter's difficulty in making friends, Barton's parents sent her to boarding school. They hoped that it would make her more comfortable with her peers. *Unfortunately*, it had the opposite effect. Barton lost her appetite and cried constantly. After only one term, she was brought home. From age 11 to 13, Barton stayed out of school to nurse her older brother through

---

1821年巴顿出生于一个开明的、思想自由的家庭。她比其他四个哥哥和姐姐小得多，他们很高兴在数学和阅读上辅导她。结果在她三岁入学时，巴顿已经能够阅读，做简单的算数，并会拼写三个音节的单词。她在学习上很容易追得上比她大的孩子，但是在交际方面还是不适应。

考虑到他们女儿在交朋友方面的困难，巴顿的父母送她去寄宿学校。他们期望这样能使女儿和其他同龄人相处得更融洽些。不幸的是，结果恰恰相反。巴顿没了食欲，并总是哭。仅一学期巴顿就被接回了家。从11岁到13岁，巴顿辍学回家护理受伤严重的哥哥。在天花病爆发期间，她自愿

---

freethinking *adj.* 思想自由的   arithmetic *n.* 算数
academically *adv.* 学术地   unfortunately *adv.* 不幸地

a serious injury. She *volunteered* her time tutoring children and caring for poor families during a *smallpox* outbreak.

Barton was 40 years old and working in the U.S. Patent Office in Washington, D.C., when the Civil War broke out in 1861. The sight of wounded soldiers touched her deeply. She began to collect and distribute food, bandages, medicines, and other supplies for the Union army. Barton risked her life to transport wagonloads of supplies to the front lines. There, with little concern for her own safety, she cooked meals, assisted surgeons, and comforted wounded soldiers, even as bullets *whizzed* around her.

Eventually the stress and toil took its toll. Barton *collapsed*, ill with typhoid fever. When she recovered, her doctors prescribed a long,

---

辅导孩子学习，照顾可怜的家人。

1861年内战爆发时，40岁的巴顿在美国华盛顿的商务部专利局工作。她目睹了受伤的战士，这深深地触动了她。她开始为联邦军队收集并分发食品、绑带、药以及其他军需品。巴顿冒着生命危险向前线运送物资。在那里她却很少关心自己的安危，甚至当子弹在她周围盘旋时，她仍然蒸煮食物、辅助手术、安慰受伤的战士。

慢慢地压力和疲劳最终让她付出了代价。巴顿倒下了，生病伴着伤寒高烧。当她醒过来时，医生叮嘱她去欧洲度一个长假，好好休息。在那儿

---

volunteer *v.* 自愿
whizz *v.* 嗖嗖地移动

smallpox *n.* 天花
collapse *v.* 晕倒；倒下

restful trip to Europe. It was there that she learned of an organization based in Switzerland—called the International Red Cross—whose work mirrored her own.

Shortly after Barton arrived back home in 1873, her sister died, and Barton fell into a deep *depression*. While *recuperating* at a health *facility* in New York, she began planning and *lobbying* for the establishment of an American wing of the International Red Cross. Although at first the government resisted, Barton's efforts finally paid off. The American Red Cross was officially organized on May 21, 1881. Her influence lives on today in the work of the organization she founded.

她了解了一个以瑞士为基地的组织——国际红十字会——这个组织的工作正是她所做的一切。

1873年巴顿回家后不久，她的姐姐死了，这使得巴顿很失落。当她在纽约的一个健康机构休养时，她开始计划并游说建立国际红十字会的美国分支。虽然起先政府反对，但巴顿的努力最终得到了收获。1881年5月21日，美国红十字会正式成立。今天她的影响依然活在她所创立的组织的工作中。

---

depression *n.* 失落
facility *n.* 场所

recuperate *v.* 休养
lobby *v.* 游说

5

A Woman with a Flare for Success

When her inventor husband died in 1848, Martha Coston, at the age of 21, became a *widow* with four children to support and little money. Eleven years later, she would patent an invention that would help win the Civil War. Coston's drive and talent placed her among history's most *accomplished* women.

以照明弹成功的女人

在1848年当她的发明家丈夫去世时，21岁的玛莎·考斯通成为了一个寡妇，有四个孩子需要抚养，但几乎没有钱。11年后，她取得了一项发明的专利，这项发明也将帮助内战取胜。考斯通的动力和天赋使她进入历史上最有成就的女人之列。

---

widow *n.* 寡妇   accomplished *adj.* 才华高的；技艺高超的

Shortly after her husband's death, Coston, sorting through papers, found plans for a type of *flare* that ships could use to communicate with one another at night. In dire need of income, Coston sent samples to the U.S. Navy for testing. The Navy *acknowledged* that the idea was great. However, it reported that Coston's flares did not work.

Coston *refined* her husband's design. With no business or science experience, she directed a team of chemists as they devised formulas and conducted experiments. Finally, her design was successful. She patented her red, white, and green "*pyrotechnic* night signals" in 1859. Two years later, she sold the patent to the Navy but received only $20,000, a fraction of its value.

考斯通在她丈夫死后不久，在分类文件时发现了一种照明弹的制作计划，船只在夜晚可以用这种照明弹相互联系。因为急需收入，考斯通把样品寄给美国海军用于测试。海军承认这个设想很好。然而测试报告称考斯通的照明弹没起到作用。

考斯通改良了她丈夫的设计。在没有商业和科学经验的情况下，她指导了一队化学家设计配方和进行实验。最终她的设计成功了。在1859年她取得了红、白、绿"烟火夜间信号弹"的专利权。两年后她把专利权卖给美国海军，但仅获得了两万美元，这只是它价值的一小部分。

---

flare *n.* 照明弹
refine *v.* 完善

acknowledge *v.* 承认
pyrotechnic *adj.* 烟火的

In 1861 the Civil War broke out. Coston's factory churned out thousands of signal flares but was paid only their cost by the Navy. The flares played an important role in the capture of *blockade* runners, boats that tried to sneak past Union blockades of *Confederate* ports.

在1861年内战爆发。考斯通的工厂艰苦地做出几千枚信号照明弹，但美国海军仅付了制作成本。在阻断逃跑者的抓捕中，以及在围堵试图溜过同盟军港口的联合封锁的船只中，照明弹起到了极其重要的作用。

blockade *n.* 封锁   confederate *n.* 同盟；同谋

6

Australian Aborigines: Living with a Land and a Legacy

The people known as Australian aborigines were the first human beings on the continent of Australia. (The word *aborigine* means "from the beginning" in Latin.) Arriving at least 40,000 years ago, they occupied most of the continent some 10,000 years later.

The climate was harsh. *Sweltering* heat

澳大利亚土著居民：与土地和遗产共生存

被称为澳大利亚土著居民的人是最初来到澳大利亚这片大陆上的人。（"土著"这个词在拉丁语中意思是"从开始起"。）他们在至少是四万年前来到这里，在其后的一万年里，他们占据了这片大陆的大部分地区。

这里的气候非常严酷。让人透不过气来的闷热和周期性的干旱不利于

---

aborigine *n.* 土著居民　　　　　　　　sweltering *adj.* 酷热难耐的

and *periodic* droughts were *unfavorable* to the growth of crops. Also, there were no native herd animals that could be tamed and used to plow the land. As a result, the aborigines led a *nomadic* life and did not acquire many possessions. Their tools had to be portable or *makeshift* (used in one place and then abandoned). One of their tools, the boomerang, is unique among early tools. Although other early hunter-gatherers threw sticks to bring down game, the boomerang's aerodynamic shape ensured that it would return to the thrower if it failed to hit its target.

Another major influence on the aboriginal way of life was the people's mythology. These beliefs spelled out the laws by which they lived and their ideals of harmony and equality. The aborigines believed that their ancestors, mythical beings, created the world

---

农作物的生长。而且当地没有能够被驯服的畜群动物用来犁地。结果,土著居民过起了游牧生活,没有获得很多财产。他们的工具必须是便携式的或者是临时凑合的(在一个地方用完然后就丢掉了)。回飞棒是他们工具中的一种,这种工具在早期工具中很独特。尽管其他早期的狩猎收集者也扔棒子去打倒猎物,但回飞棒动力学的形状确保它在没有击中目标时,返回到投掷者那里。

另外一个主要影响土著居民生活方式的是人们的神话。这些信仰显示了他们生存的法律准则,以及他们追求和谐与平等的理想。土著居民认

---

periodic *adj.* 周期性的   unfavorable *adj.* 不利的

nomadic *adj.* 游牧的   makeshift *adj.* 临时凑合的

and everything in it—land, plants, animals, and people—during "the dreaming". These beings passed along their *legacy*, known as "the dreamtime", to their *descendants*. This *bequest* was made known through the dreams of certain revered old men. The aborigines believed that their purpose in life was to live in agreement with this legacy—in harmony with it, the land, and its *inhabitants*, rather than in competition with others.

Early aborigines lived in social groups determined by their beliefs and the land itself. Because of the harsh climate and the aborigines' nomadic lifestyle, they lived in small bands rather than large settlements. Their mythology connected them to a certain region of land as well as to the plants and animals found there. This resulted in aborigines' living in "estate groups" that were generally related

---

为他们的祖先是神话中的人物，祖先在"梦中"创造了世界以及世上万物（陆地、植物、动物和人）。这些先人把被称为"梦幻时光"的遗产传给他们的后人。这份遗产通过受人尊敬的老人们的梦而知名。土著居民认为他们生活的目的就是生活得与这份遗产保持一致——与它和谐相处，包括陆地和居民，而不是与其他人竞争。

　　早期的土著居民生活在由他们的信仰和土地本身所决定的社会部落里。因为恶劣的气候和土著居民游牧的生活方式，他们以小队生活在一起，而不是大规模的定居。他们的神话把他们和陆上的特定区域，以及在

---

legacy *n.* 遗产　　　　　　　　　　　descendant *n.* 后代
bequest *n.* 遗产　　　　　　　　　　 inhabitant *n.* 居民

on the male side. The males in the group were the *guardians* of the "*estate*". They engaged in sacred *rites* and *rituals* intended to renew and sustain the land and its inhabitants. There was no centralized leadership or government, nor were aborigines divided into social classes. Instead, they relied on their belief in their legacy, and their need to live in agreement with their ancestors' wishes, to ensure that group members lived in accordance with society's rules and in harmony with one another.

那发现的植物和动物联系在一起。这就导致土著居民生活在"财产团体"里，而这都是与男性有关的。在团体中男性是"财产"的保护者。他们举行神圣的仪式和典礼，目的是更新和维持这片土地和它的居民。这里没有中央集权的领导者或者政府，土著居民也没有被分成社会等级。相反，他们依赖他们遗产中的信仰，他们需要在生活中与他们祖先的愿望保持一致，以确保团体成员们生活中遵守社会规则，与其他人和谐相处。

---

guardian *n.* 保护者；保卫者
rite *n.* 仪式

estate *n.* 财产
ritual *n.* 宗教仪式；典礼

7

Early Tools and Toolmaking

In its earliest stages, technology consisted of toolmaking. The Paleolithic period has three *subdivisions*. Each is defined by changes in human toolmaking.

During the Lower Paleolithic period (150 thousand to 2.5 million years ago), a *pebble* might be used for pounding, digging,

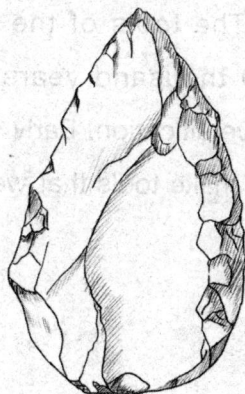

早期的工具和工具制造

在最早期阶段，科技包括工具制造。旧石器时代分为三个阶段，每一个阶段都是以人类工具制造的变化而界定的。

在旧石器时代早期（15万年到250万年前），一块卵石就可以用来敲打、挖掘或刮擦，或者一块大的石头就可以用来击碎一块易碎的岩石，从

---

subdivision *n.* 分支；分部

pebble *n.* 卵石

or scraping, or a large stone might be struck against an easily splintered rock, producing sharpedged flakes for cutting.

An important tool appeared during the Middle Paleolithic period (40 thousand to 150 thousand years ago). It was the *symmetrical* hand *ax*. A bone hammer was employed to administer a series of precise strikes that resulted in a carefully chiseled disk. The toolmaker had to be intelligent to create such a tool.

The tools of the Upper Paleolithic period (10 thousand to 40 thousand years ago) were *characterized* by *portability* and diversification. Early hunters carried "tool kits". They used the kits to make tools that were suited to a variety of purposes. They made

---

而产生可以用来切东西的有着锋利边缘的薄石片。

一件重要的工具出现在旧石器时代中期（4万年到15万年前）。这就是对称的手斧。把一个骨锤进行一系列精确的敲打，就制成了一个轮廓分明的盘状物。工具制造工一定是很聪慧的，才可以制作出这么一种工具。

旧石器时代晚期（1万年到4万年前）的工具是以便于携带和多样化为特征的。早期的猎人带着"工具装备"。他们使用工具装备来制作适合

---

symmetrical *adj.* 对称的
characterize *v.* 表示……的特征

ax *n.* 斧子
portability *n.* 可携带性

projectiles, scrapers for cleaning hides, borers, and burins (*engravers*) to decorate bone. One very important *innovation* was the spear thrower, a simple device still in use by Australian aborigines. This weapon extended the human arm's range and force. The extension helped early people to hunt migrating animals successfully.

多种用途的工具。他们制作抛射物、清理兽皮的刮刀、钻孔器，以及用来装饰骨头的雕刻刀。一个非常重要的革新是投掷矛，这种简单的工具仍然被澳大利亚土著居民使用。这件武器扩大了人类手臂的使用范围和力量，帮助了早期的人类成功猎捕移动中的动物。

engraver *n.* 雕刻师；雕工   innovation *n.* 革新

8

John F. Kennedy: Soft on Civil Rights?

John F. Kennedy took office as president of the United States in 1961. At that time, African Americans' struggle for civil rights was reaching its *peak*. Kennedy's response to the crisis was mixed. Many historians believe that political concerns made him limit his support of civil rights protections for *minorities*.

约翰·F·肯尼迪：在民权问题上软弱？

1961 年约翰·F·肯尼迪就职美国总统。那时，美国黑人对于民权的斗争正达到高潮。肯尼迪对于这次危机的回答很模糊。许多历史学家认为，出于政治上的考虑使他减少了他对少数人民权保护的支持。

---

peak *n.* 高峰　　　　　　　　　　　　　minority *n.* 少数人

One of Kennedy's *campaign* promises was to end *discrimination* in public housing. He would do so, he said, by executive order, "with the stroke of a pen." This promise helped him to win almost three-quarters of the African American vote. After he took office, however, many found his actions in support of civil rights to be less than expected. Kennedy, a *Democrat*, had only a slight majority in Congress. He believed that by pushing the cause of civil rights, he would lose the support of Southern Democrats. When he still had not signed the promised order after two years, civil rights supporters reminded him of his pledge by sending pens to the White House.

Kennedy planned to introduce civil rights *legislation* in his second term. By that time, he believed, most of his program would have

---

　　肯尼迪竞选活动的其中一个承诺就是结束公共住房的歧视问题。他说他会这样做，"大笔一挥"，使用行政命令。这项承诺帮他赢得了美国黑人中几乎四分之三的选票。然而，在他就职之后，许多人发现他并没有像所期望的那样支持民权运动。肯尼迪，一个民主党人，在国会中只得到了略多于一半人的支持。他认为推行民权将会使他失去南方民主党人的支持。两年后他仍然没有履行承诺，民权的支持者用一种往白宫寄送钢笔的方法提醒他所立的誓言。

　　肯尼迪计划在他的第二任期推出民权立法。他相信，到那时他的多

---

campaign *n.* 竞选　　　　　　discrimination *n.* 歧视
Democrat *n.* 美国民主党人；民主主义者　　legislation *n.* 立法

been passed. However, events in his first term forced him to take direct action. In 1962 an African American student *enrolled* at the University of Mississippi for the first time in its history. Rioting broke out on campus, and Kennedy sent 3 thousand federal troops to restore order. The following year, Kennedy put the Alabama National Guard under federal authority. The guards were to control the *rioting* and ensure that African Americans would be allowed to enroll in public universities throughout the state. In a speech shortly after these events, he declared to Congress, "It ought to be possible ... for every American to enjoy the *privileges* of being American without regard to his race or his color."

Congress took up the challenge and began debate on a civil rights

---

数计划都会被通过。然而，在他第一任期内发生的事请迫使他采取直接行动。在1962年，一位美国黑人学生登记入学密西西比大学，这在历史上是第一次。暴乱在校园里爆发，肯尼迪派出了三千人的联邦军队恢复秩序。第二年，肯尼迪在联邦政府下设立了阿拉巴马州国民警卫队。警卫队用来控制暴乱并确保美国黑人被允许进入全国的公立大学。在这些事件发生不久后的一次演讲中，他对国会宣布，"这应该是可能的……对于每一位美国人都要享有作为美国人的权利，不论种族还是肤色。"

国会接纳了这项挑战并且开始对这项议案进行讨论；但是直到1963

---

enrol *v.* 注册　　　　　　　　　　　　　　　　rioting *n.* 暴乱
privilege *n.* 特权

bill; but when Kennedy was *assassinated* in November 1963, the bill had not yet been passed. Although Kennedy's successor, Lyndon Baines Johnson, supported it, debate in Congress was heated. *Opponents* attempted to kill the bill with a 75-day *filibuster*, a debate designed to cause delay. In 1964, however, Johnson signed the Civil Rights Act into law. The law protects the rights of minorities to vote and have free access to public facilities. The Civil Rights Act of 1964 stands today as one of the strongest U.S. civil rights laws.

年11月肯尼迪遇刺时,这项议案还没有通过。尽管肯尼迪的继任者林登·贝恩斯·约翰逊支持这项议案,但是在国会中仍然有激烈的争议。反对者试图用75天的阻挠来扼杀这项议案,即通过争论来把这件事拖延下来。然而在1964年,约翰逊签署了民权法。这项法案维护了少数人的选举权和公共设施的自由使用权。1964年民权法案对于今天来说仍然是美国最有影响力的民权法律之一。

---

assassinate *v.* 暗杀   opponent *n.* 反对者
filibuster *n.* 阻挠

9

Bringing History Back to the White House

Shortly after her husband had been selected president, Jacqueline Kennedy was taken on a visit to the White House. She was *aghast*. Long *fascinated* with the history of the *presidency*, she believed that as an American treasure the White House deserved care and impressive *presentation*.

把历史带回白宫

在丈夫被选为总统后不久,杰奎琳·肯尼迪就参观了白宫。她为所看到的感到震惊。她被总统的历史深深地吸引,她相信作为美国的国宝,白宫应得到精心的照料,以及进行令人印象深刻的的展示。

---

aghast *adj.* 惊骇的
presidency *n.* 总统职位(或任期等)

fascinated *adj.* 入迷的
presentation *n.* 展示;出示

The First Lady went to work to restore the public rooms to their original *appearance*, organizing the White House Fine Arts *Committee* to carry out the work. She also established the White House Historical *Association*, which published the first-ever White House guidebook. The committee used profits from the sale of the book to locate historical treasures that were in collections throughout the country.

Mrs. Kennedy always stressed that her work was much more than redecorating. The effort was a work of "*scholarship*", she said. Returning possessions of presidents such as Washington, Lincoln, and Madison to the White House was one of the committee's greatest successes.

　　这位第一夫人立即着手把公共房间恢复到它们最初面貌的工作，她组织白宫艺术委员会来实施这项工作。她还建立了白宫历史协会，出版了第一本白宫旅游指南，委员会用卖书赚来的钱搜集全国有历史价值的宝藏。

　　肯尼迪夫人一直强调，她的工作不仅仅是重新修复。她说，所做的努力是增长"学识"的一项工作。把这些总统的所有物品，例如华盛顿、林肯和麦迪逊，送回到白宫，是委员会最大的成功之一。

---

appearance *n.* 外观；外表
association *n.* 协会

committee *n.* 委员会
scholarship *n.* 学问成就

However, Mrs. Kennedy did not stop at *restoration*. She made the White House a living center of the arts by welcoming leading artists, writers, and *entertainers*. The White House, she thought, should serve not only as the seat of political power in the United States but also as one of the country's chief cultural centers. The tradition she began 40 years ago continues to this day.

　　然而，肯尼迪夫人没有停止在修复工作上。通过邀请那些主要的艺术家、作家和演艺人员，她把白宫变成了一个充满活力的艺术中心。她认为白宫不应该只是美国的政治权力所在地，而且还应该是国家的主要文化中心。她在40年前开始的传统一直延续到今天。

---

restoration *n.* 恢复   entertainer *n.* 表演者

10

Film and the Depression

In October 1929, the U.S. *stock* market crashed, ushering in the Great *Depression*. At that time, film as a form of entertainment was fairly new. The first "talkie", or movie with sound, *The Jazz Singer*, had been released two years earlier. Like any young industry, film was *undergoing*

大萧条时期的电影产业

1929年10月，美国股票市场崩盘，使美国进入经济大萧条时期。在当时，电影作为一种娱乐形式正处于萌芽期。第一部有声电影《爵士歌手》也已于两年前发行。正如众多新兴产业，电影业也经历着巨大改变。尤其在电影制片人考虑广大观众的品味和

---

stock *n.* 股票   depression *n.* 萧条期
undergo *v.* 经历

changes. These changes became more *pronounced* as filmmakers reflected the tastes and concerns of their viewers.

The Depression filled Americans with despair and *shattered* their trust in the social system. Bread lines and soup kitchens fed hungry citizens. Desperate workers struggled to earn pennies by *hawking* apples on the streets. The films of the early 1930s reflected these harsh realities. *Exploitation*, a common theme, was portrayed in romantic relationships, work, and law. Characters used immoral and ruthless means to get the better of one another. Stock roles included the fallen woman, the forgotten man, the abandoned youth, the greedy capitalist, and oppressed workers. Topics related to social chaos and the evils of class inequity were the norm in dramas and comedies. Gangster films, in which "bad guys" not only starred but

---

偏好时，这种改变显得尤为显著。

萧条期令美国人失望，同时也摧毁了他们对社会体系的信任。饥饿的市民唯有以面包和汤充饥。为生活所迫的工人不得不在大街上以兜售苹果为生。20世纪30年代早期的电影就反映了这时期残酷的现实生活。剥削这一普遍的主题，在浪漫的关系，工作和法律中被描绘出来。演员也运用不道德的及残酷的方式很好地再现了芸芸众生：股票持有人包括堕落的妇女、被忽略的男人、放纵的年轻人、贪婪的资本家还有受压迫的工人。与混乱的社会状态和阶级不平等的邪恶相关的主题在戏剧和喜剧作品中被定为标准。以歹徒为主题的电影中不仅由"恶劣的家伙"担任主角，这样的

---

pronounced *adj.* 明显的
hawk *v.* （沿街）兜售

shatter *v.* 粉碎；严重打击
exploitation *n.* 剥削

also often came out on top, were among the most popular films of the early 1930s.

People seemed to enjoy this steely view of life. But some groups saw this trend as dangerous. In 1933 the Roman Catholic Church's Legion of Decency threatened to organize *boycotts* of any film it judged to be *immoral*. Hollywood responded by setting up a production code in 1934. Films began to tell stories of *wholesomeness*. Law officers, such as the Western sheriff, replaced gangsters as heroes. Wealth was no longer an evil but a *supreme* good.

This mood shift spawned a new genre of film—the screwball comedy. Sexuality was now expressed through clever wordplay as men and women revealed their attraction for one another in comic

---

电影还经常跻身于电影榜首，成为20世纪30年代早期最受欢迎的电影。

人们似乎很喜欢电影中这种严酷的生命视角，但一些人认为这种趋势极其危险。在1933年，罗马天主教教会团体威胁并组织抵制那些不道德的电影。而好莱坞也于1934年制定了电影出品法规予以回应。电影开始讲述有关有益身心健康为主题的故事。诸如西部行政司法长官等法律官员，作为英雄形象来代替歹徒角色。财富不再是邪恶与不幸的代名词，而是一种至高无上的物品。

这种情感的转变使怪诞喜剧作为一种新的电影类型涌现。男女之间彼

---

boycott *n.* 联合抵制
wholesomeness *n.* 有益身心健康

immoral *adj.* 不道德的
supreme *adj.* 至上的

battles. The rich were no longer *portrayed* as exploiting the poor. Now they were *carefree* and *wacky*; and if they made mistakes that hurt those less fortunate, it was not from greed but from *ignorance*. Happy endings, in which such characters saw the error of their ways and were rewarded with true love, money, or both, were essential to the formula. What films lost in dealing frankly with the more troubling side of life they gained in a new set of fresh, amusing ways to offer hope that the American dream really was within reach of every American.

此显露爱慕后通过在对话中的巧妙的俏皮话含蓄地表达性欲。在电影中，富人不再扮演压迫利用穷人的角色。他们变得不关世事又怪僻。假如他们无意伤害了那些不幸的人，也不是出自贪欲而是出于无知。结局都是以主角意识到他们的过错，并以金钱或真爱或用这两者来弥补过失美好收场的，这都是电影规则所要求的。尽管电影在处理令人烦恼的生活方面失去了坦诚，但它们还是以一种新颖有趣的方式为美国人提供希望，即每一个美国人都能实现自己的美国梦。

---

portray *v.* 描写　　　　　　　　　　carefree *adj.* 无忧无虑的
wacky *adj.* 怪僻的　　　　　　　　　ignorance *n.* 无知

11

Edison's Kinetoscope and the Birth of the Movies

Thomas Alva Edison *demonstrated* his *kinetoscope* in 1893. The device was both a camera and a viewer. It looked like a small *cabinet* with a viewing lens mounted on top. The film ran *horizontally* past the lens. This device made Edison a pioneer in the motion-picture industry. Later it became one of the world's most popular forms of

爱迪生的电影放映机和电影的诞生

在1893年，托马斯·阿尔瓦·爱迪生展示了他的电影放映机。这个装置既是摄影机又是观看器。它看起来像一个小型的上面带有观看镜头的橱柜。电影透过镜头横向放映。这个设备使爱迪生在电影行

---

demonstrate *v.* 展示   kinetoscope *n.* 电影放映机
cabinet *n.* 橱柜   horizontally *adv.* 水平地

entertainment.

In 1893 Edison opened a studio in West Orange, New Jersey. There, a team produced the world's first movies. These short films included actualities, advertisements, dramas and comedies, tricks, and reenactments. Kinetoscope parlors soon sprouted up in cities and began to show these films.

The first films were actualities, *nonfiction snippets* that provided *glimpses* of famous people, places, and events. The first actualities showed boxers, dancers, clowns, and other performers. After a portable camera was developed, the studio produced films of city and nature scenes, train travel, and news events. One of the

业成为首创者。后来它成为世界最受欢迎的娱乐形式之一。

在1893年，爱迪生在新泽西州的西橙摄影棚开设了一个电影工作室。在那里，一个团队制作出了世界第一部电影。这些短电影包括实景、广告、戏剧和喜剧、滑稽剧、翻拍剧。电影放映机业务室在城市间迅速发展并开始放映这些电影。

最初的影片是现实剧、纪实文学作品片段，提供欣赏名人名胜和著名的事件。第一批现实剧包括拳击运动员、舞蹈演员、小丑和其他表演者。在便携式的摄影机出现之后，这间摄影棚制作出了展现城市和自然景

nonfiction *n.* 纪实文学　　　　　　　　　　　　　snippet *n.* 片断
glimpse *n.* 一瞥

most *renowned* showed the 1897 swearing in of President William McKinley. Another showed the "burial" of the battleship U.S.S. Maine, sunk in the Spanish-American War.

Starting in 1913, Edison began to work on a device called a kinetophone that could match sound to films. However, he never perfected the kinetophone. It was *abandoned* two years later. Soon Edison dropped out of the film industry.

色，火车旅行和新闻事件的电影。最著名的一个影片展现了1897年的美国总统威廉·麦金莱的宣誓。另外一个影片展现了美国军舰缅因号的"葬礼"，即它在美西战争中的沉没。

从1913年开始，爱迪生开始研究一种能把声音和电影相配套的放映机。然而他没能完成，两年后就放弃了。很快爱迪生退出了电影业。

---

renowned *adj.* 有名的

abandon *v.* 放弃

12

The Genius of Ancient Rome

In the sixth century B.C., Rome was a minor town in central Italy. Only a few centuries later, it was a *bustling* city at the center of one of the most powerful empires in history. In its *prime*, Rome *commanded* an empire that ringed the Mediterranean. The Roman Empire included England, much of Europe, most of Asia,west of the Euphrates

古罗马的天赋

公元前6世纪，罗马是位于意大利中部的一个小镇。仅仅过了几个世纪，它就成为了历史上最强大帝国之一的繁荣的中心城市。当罗马发展到鼎盛时期时，它便要求在地中海地区建立一个帝国。罗马帝国包括英格兰、欧洲的大部分地区、亚洲的大部分地区、幼发拉底河西部、非洲北部，还包括领域内所有的岛屿。为什么罗马会成为历史上最

---

bustling *adj.* 繁荣的
command *v.* 要求

prime *n.* 全盛时期

River, northern Africa, and all of the islands in between. Why did Rome emerge as one of the greatest powers of all times? There are several related reasons.

To forge an empire, a nation needs vast armies that can fight on *numerous* fronts. Unlike its neighbors, Rome made it a practice to grant citizenship to any non-Romans joining their cause. They also let all citizens share in the spoils of victory. Such an open-door policy created a steady flow of enlistees who had a stake in the *outcome* of battle. In addition, the Romans developed an open formation of small groups of soldiers, which had two great advantages. Troops could quickly be *mobilized* and deployed as needed. *Substitutions* of fresh soldiers could readily be made for dead or wounded ones.

强大的帝国之一呢？有几个相关原因。

　　要造就帝国，这个国家就需要大批的能够在许多前线作战的军队。与邻国不同，罗马制定了一个惯例，即授予任何加入他们的非罗马人罗马公民身份。他们也让所有的市民分享胜利后的战利品。这种开放政策使罗马有了稳定的士兵来源，士兵可以获得战争成果的奖金。而且，罗马建立了小团体士兵的开放编队，这种体系有两个优点：首先，当有需要时，能很快地组织和部署军队。其次，能够准备新兵来代替死伤人员。

numerous *adj.* 大量的
mobilize *v.* 调动

outcome *n.* 结果
substitution *n.* 代替

Once a region came under Roman control, it could go about its business under the authority of a *provincial* governor. The Romans found it *efficient* to have their empire *administered* at the local level, rather than concentrating power in Rome. This was not the case with their legal system, however. The Romans unified a jumble of ancient laws and practices into a *coherent* whole. No longer was the law subject to a variety of interpretations depending upon who was judging and who was being judged. Rather, the law was predictable and was applied in the same way throughout the empire. The Roman system of governance created stability and produced, through heavy taxation, a steady stream of riches to Rome.

In order to maintain the empire's infrastructure, the ancient Romans focused on building useful structures. They built bridges,

---

一旦一个地区被罗马控制，它将会在地方政府的管辖下进行各种事务。罗马人发现以地方机构来管理他们的帝国，而不是把权力集中在罗马的方法很有效。然而，这并不是他们法律体系的一部分。罗马人把混乱而古老的法律和现实统一成一个整体。因此，法律不再依靠那些由判决的人和被判决的人所做出的解释。然而，法律是可预见的，并且以同样的方式被运用到整个帝国。通过繁重的赋税，稳定的财富流入到罗马，罗马的管理体系表现出稳定性和有效性。

为了维护帝国的基础设施，古罗马人把重点放到建造有用的建筑上。他们建桥、大仓库和能把水送到公共场所的导水管。他们也建公寓、公共

---

provincial *adj.* 地方的
administer *v.* 管理

efficient *adj.* 高效的
coherent *adj.* 连贯的

huge *warehouses*, and *aqueducts* that carried water to the public. They also built apartment buildings, public baths, *sewers*, and paved roads on which goods or armies could be transported. The Romans' creation of cement was important to their *architecture*. This substance proved to be far stronger than other building materials of the time.

If the ancient Greeks were brilliant creators and visionary idealists, the ancient Romans were expert technicians and tacticians. They were, in a word, practical.

浴池、下水道和供运输货物和军队的专行道。罗马人水泥的发明对罗马的建筑学起着重要的作用。这种物质证明要远远比同时期的其他建筑材料更坚固。

如果古希腊人是杰出的创造者和有远见的理想主义者，那么古罗马人就是技术专家和战略家。简言之，他们都是务实的。

---

warehouse *n.* 仓库
sewer *n.* 下水道

aqueduct *n.* 引水渠；导水管
architecture *n.* 建筑学

13

Augustus and the Pax Romana

In 45 B.C., Roman emperor Julius Caesar adopted his 18-year-old greatnephew Octavian as his son and *heir*. One year later, the young man was *fatherless*. Caesar's enemies had murdered him. In the years after Caesar's death, Octavian, Marc Antony (Caesar's second in command), and a man named Lepidus

奥古斯都与罗马和平

公元前45年，罗马统治者朱利叶斯·凯撒收养了他18岁的侄孙屋大维（即奥古斯都）为儿子和继承人。一年之后，这位年轻人的父亲凯撒便去世了。凯撒的反对者谋杀了他。在凯撒去世后的几年里，屋大维，马克·安东尼（凯撒的副指挥官）和一个名叫雷比达的人共同统

---

heir *n.* 继承人　　　　　　　　　　fatherless *adj.* 没有父亲的

ruled. Gaining *poise* and military strength, Octavian *wrested* control first from Lepidus (32 B.C.) and then from Antony (31 B.C.).

Luckily for Rome, Octavian did not plan to build a military *dictatorship*. Instead, Caesar's heir proved more than equal to the task of governing. He restored order to Rome, *dismantled* his army, and called for regular elections. Predictably, he was elected consul. He offered to give up his powers, but the Roman Senate rejected his offer. Instead, they bestowed honors upon him. Among them was the title of Augustus, meaning "honored". He soon became known by this name.

Augustus took a Rome that had been in disarray and rebuilt its

---

治罗马。为了使权利平衡并且增强军事力量，屋大维先于公元前32年夺取了雷比达的政权，然后在公元前31年夺取了安东尼的政权。

对于罗马来说幸运的是，屋大维并没有计划建立一个军事独裁的国家政权。相反，凯撒的继承人证明了不仅仅是平等的统治任务。他恢复了罗马的秩序，解散了他的军队并且呼吁以正规的方式进行选举。不出所料，他当选为执政官。他曾经提出放弃他的权力，但是罗马参议院拒绝了这项提议。并且，他们授予了他很多荣誉。在那些荣誉中便有一个称号是奥古斯都，意为"受人尊敬的"。很快，他的这个名字便众所周知。

奥古斯都使混乱的罗马重建了政府、传统以及建筑。在他的统治下，

---

poise *n.* 平衡

dictatorship *n.* 独裁政府

wrest *v.* 攫取；抢夺

dismantle *v.* 解散

government, its traditions, and its architecture. Under his rule, the empire expanded and united. The Mediterranean world entered a period of *harmony* and wealth that became known as the Pax Romana (Latin for "Roman peace"). This period lasted for more than 200 years. Augustus died in A.D. 14. Many considered him one of the great *administrative* geniuses of history.

罗马帝国扩张了领土并且使之团结在一起。地中海地区进入了一个和谐且富有的时代，这一时期被称为罗马帝国统治下的和平时期（"Roman peace"的拉丁语）。这一时期持续了200多年。奥古斯都死于公元14年。很多人都评价他是历史上最伟大的管理天才之一。

harmony *n.* 和谐   administrative *adj.* 管理的

14

Haves and Have-Nots in the 1950s

Many Americans think of the 1950s as a time of *poodle* skirts, sock hops, two-car garages, soda fountains, tidy suburbs, and *wholesome* values. With good jobs and money in the bank, many people enjoyed a good lifestyle. But these images make up only part of the 1950s scene. The other side of the *landscape* was not quite so

20世纪50年代的拥有与匮乏

许多美国人把20世纪50年代看做这样一个时代，这个时代满是长鬈毛裙、短袜舞会、双车车库、冷饮小卖部、整洁的郊区以及有益身心的价值观。许多人有好工作，有钱可以存到银行，他们喜欢这种好的生活方式。但是这些场景仅仅是20世纪50年代社会场景的一部分，

---

poodle *n.* 卷毛狗
landscape *n.* 风景

wholesome *adj.* 有益于身心健康的

attractive.

During the decade, the country's *gross* national product grew by 51 percent. This bull economy was fueled by several factors, including defense spending. Fears of nuclear *devastation* and global communist *takeovers propelled* the Cold War, and the Cold War propelled defense spending. Under President Dwight D. Eisenhower, the U.S. government pumped about $350 billion into defense.

Automation—the development of machines to do jobs once done by hand—changed the workforce. Also, many soldiers returning from World War II took advantage of the GI bill. This was a special government program to pay for college tuition. Returning soldiers

---

而另一部分就不那么吸引人了。

在整个十年期间，国家的国民生产总值增长51％。庞大的经济被诸多因素推动着，包括国防花销。对核破坏性的恐惧以及全球共产主义者的接管推进了冷战，冷战又推进了国防花销。在德怀特·戴维·艾森豪威尔当总统期间，美国政府将大约3500亿美元投入到国防中。

自动化（机器的发展用以完成曾经用手完成的工作）改变了劳动力。一些从二战返回来的士兵也从退伍军人法案中得到了好处。这是一个用来支付大学学费的特殊的政府项目。这些回来的士兵渴望得到白领的工作。自动化废除了一些蓝领的工作，但是工厂工人的工资提高了50％。

---

gross *adj.* 总的

takeover *n.* 接管

devastation *n.* 毁坏

propel *v.* 推进

were eager to fill the growing number of white-collar jobs. *Automation* did away with many blue-collar jobs, but wages for factory workers rose by 50 percent.

These workers, both blue collar and white collar, joined the middle class. They married and had many children, setting the 18-year period of high birth rates after World War II, known as the baby boom, into motion. Adults were glad that the *hardships* of the Great Depression and the war years were over. Their children, many of whom had never experienced going without whatever they needed, shared their hunger for *consumer* goods.

But America had a troubling secret—poverty. Political activist Michael Harrington brought this fact to light in his 1962 book, *The Other America*. Harrington *estimated* that 50 million Americans

---

蓝领工人和白领工人都加入到了中产阶级行列里。他们结了婚并且生了许多孩子，使二战之后高出生率持续了18年的时间，这段时期被称为婴儿潮。令成年人高兴的是，大萧条期的困苦以及多年的战争结束了。他们的孩子当中，有许多没有经历过需要无法得到满足的生活，分享他们想得到的消费品。

但是美国有一个令人烦恼的秘密——贫穷。政治活动家迈克尔·哈林顿在他1962年的《另一个美国》一书中揭露了这个事实。哈林顿估计有5 000万美国人生活在贫穷当中。大多数人绝没有看见过这些"其他的美国人"，但是敢于远离绿色的郊区和闪闪发光的市中心的人就会看到。

---

automation *n.* 自动化
consumer *n.* 消费

hardship *n.* 困苦的条件
estimate *v.* 估计

lived in poverty. Most people never saw these "other Americans", but anyone who *ventured* away from the grassy suburbs and shiny downtown areas did. These "other Americans" were hidden away in *backwoods hamlets* and urban *ghettoes*. While most Americans were concerned with what to buy next, the underclass lacked proper nutrition, health care, and decent housing. Unnoticed and lacking a political voice, the poor were all but invisible.

These dismal truths inspired President John F. Kennedy to assemble a task force on poverty. After Kennedy's death in 1963, his successor, Lyndon B. Johnson, took up the fight. He launched his "war on poverty", which became one of the chief hallmarks of his presidency.

这些"其他的美国人"被隐藏在偏远地区的小村和都市的贫民区。当大多数美国人关心接下来买什么的时候，下层阶级的人们却缺乏适当的营养、医疗和像样的房子。这些穷人被忽视，缺少政治上的发言权，他们只能是隐形人。

　　这些凄凉的事实鼓舞了肯尼迪总统强加给自己一项改变贫困状况的任务。在1963年约翰·F·肯尼迪死后，他的继任者林登·B·约翰逊接管了这个任务。他发起了他的"贫困之战"，这也成为了他总统任期内主要的标志性事件之一。

---

venture *v.* 冒险
hamlet *n.* 小村子

backwoods *n.* 人烟稀少的边远地带
ghetto *n.* 贫民区

15

Homelessness in the Twenty-first Century

In 2000 the United States economy dipped into economic *recession*. This caused *discomfort* and hardship in every level of society; but for many of the nation's poor, discomfort and hardship turned to misery.

A surge in *homelessness* is probably the most tragic result of a nation's financial

21世纪的无家可归者

在2000年美国陷入经济衰退。这导致社会各阶层的不适与艰难，尤其是对于这个国家的大多数穷人来说，这种不适与艰难更是雪上加霜。

对于一个国家的金融危机来说，无家可归者激增很可能是最不幸的结

recession *n.* 经济衰退   discomfort *n.* 不适
homelessness *n.* 无家可归

woes. In 2002 it was estimated that more than 3 million Americans were homeless because of a lack of *affordable* housing. Experts suggest that a family should spend no more than 30 percent of its income on housing. In contrast, in some families housing costs gobble up 50 percent or more. An unexpected event, such as missed work or illness, can quickly *plunge* a family into homelessness.

A January 2003 article in Time magazine tells the story of one such family. Until August of 2002, the young couple and their three children rented a two-bedroom apartment for about $350 a month. They *barely squeaked* by on the husband's $920-a-month take-home pay; so when their rent was raised to $500 a month, they could no

果。在2002年，估计有超过300万的美国人因为付不起房费而无家可归。专家建议，一个家庭花费在住房上的钱不应该超过收入的30%。与之形成对比的是，一些家庭花费在住房上的钱是收入的50%，甚至更多。一些意想不到的事件，比如失去工作或者是疾病，都能迅速使一个家庭陷入无家可归的状态。

　2003年1月，时代杂志刊登了一个这样的家庭的故事。直到2002年8月，这对年轻的夫妇和他们的三个孩子都在租用一个每月350美元的两室公寓。丈夫每个月920美元的工资刚刚够勉强维持他们的生活。因此当他

---

affordable *adj.* 负担得起的　　　　**plunge** *v.* 使进入
barely *adv.* 仅仅　　　　　　　　　**squeak** *v.* 勉强通过

longer make ends meet. They were lucky enough to find a three-bedroom *shelter* provided by Catholic Social Services. Although they admit the shelter is the nicest place they have ever lived, they still long for the time when they again can afford a place of their own.

们的房租涨到500美元每月时，他们不能再收支相抵。但他们是幸运的，可以找到天主教会社会服务所提供的一个三室的临时收容所。虽然他们承认这个临时收容所是他们所住过的房子中最好的，但是他们依然渴望能付得起他们自己栖身之所的日子早日到来。

---

shelter *n.* 收容所

16

I Do, I Do—in Any Tradition

Each religion has *distinctive* marriage *rituals* that honor the special relationship between a husband and a wife. Consider the different practices typical of Hinduism, Judaism, and Christianity—for example, the Greek Orthodox Church.

Hinduism is an ancient religion that developed in southern Asia about 4

不同传统中的结婚仪式

每个宗教都有为庆祝丈夫和妻子结合的有特色的结婚仪式，印度教、犹太教和基督教都有其不同的形式，还有希腊正教。

印度教是一个古老的宗教，它是在大约4000年前于亚洲南部发展起来的。犹太教在近东地区发展了几个世纪，并于2400年前结束，这是在

---

distinctive *adj.* 与众不同的；有特色的   ritual *n.* 仪式
Hinduism *n.* 印度教

thousand years ago. *Judaism* evolved in the Near East over the course of several centuries, ending about twenty-four hundred years ago, during the fifth century B.C. In the Greek Orthodox Church, which originated in Greece, a set of practices called the Byzantine rite is observed.

A traditional Hindu wedding takes place over several days and involves some social activities as well as many religious ones. A Hindu wedding may begin with an exchange of gifts of gold (often rings) and flower *garlands*. In this way, the groom and the bride welcome each other into their joint life. During the marriage ceremony, which takes place before a sacred fire, the corner of the bride's *sari*, or dress, is often *knotted* to a scarf worn by the groom. The couple's right hands are also tied together with a thread that

---

公元前5世纪期间。在起源于希腊的希腊正教里，叫做拜占庭礼的一套仪式还在被人遵从。

传统的印度婚礼像许多宗教婚礼一样要持续几天，并包括一些社会活动。印度婚礼首先以交换戒指或花环开始。以这种形式，新郎和新娘彼此欢迎对方进入他们的共同生活。婚礼仪式在圣火前举行，在婚礼仪式中，新娘莎丽或礼服的一角通常与新郎戴的围巾系在一起。新郎和新娘的右手也被一条受过祝福的线系在一起。这些动作象征着他们的结合。在曼加勒

Judaism *n.* 犹太教　　　　　　　　　　　garland *n.* 花环
sari *n.* 莎丽　　　　　　　　　　　　　　knot *v.* 打结

has been blessed. These actions *symbolize* their union. In the mangal sutra ceremony, the groom ties the *thali*, a caste symbol, around the bride's throat, recognizing her as part of his family.

In a Jewish wedding, the bride and groom stand under a *chuppah*, a little *canopy* that symbolizes the life they will build together. During the course of the ceremony, the bride and groom sip from a glass of wine—a symbol of life and a metaphor for marriage—that has been blessed. Wine starts as grape juice and eventually changes into a drink that represents joy. At the end of the service, after the couple drinks the last drops of wine, the groom crushes the empty wineglass under his heel.

经仪式中，新郎在新娘的脖子上系浅盘，这是一种种姓的象征，代表承认新娘为他家族中的一员。

在犹太婚礼中，新郎和新娘同站在一个彩棚下面，这个小遮篷象征着他们共同建立的生活。在仪式过程中新郎和新娘共同啜饮一杯酒（象征生命及暗喻婚姻），这是一杯被祝福的酒。酒刚开始通常是用葡萄汁代替，最后变成代表欢乐的一种饮料。仪式的最后，当新郎和新娘喝完最后一滴酒，新郎要用脚后跟把空酒杯踩碎。

---

symbolize *v.* 象征　　　　　　　　　　　　　　**thali** *n.* 浅盘
chuppah *n.* 婚庆典礼用的彩棚　　　　　　　　　**canopy** *n.* 罩篷

The Greek Orthodox couple does not exchange vows; the actions of the bride and groom are enough to show their *willingness* to be married. The ceremony has two parts: a *betrothal* service, when rings are exchanged, and the marriage ritual itself, during which the bride and groom are crowned with wedding crowns. These crowns are *emblems* that signify that the couple will *preside* as king and queen in the realm of their home. Toward the end of the ceremony, the couple walks around in a little circle, taking their first steps together as husband and wife.

希腊正教的新郎和新娘并不交换誓言；新郎和新娘的行动足够表明他们想要结婚的意愿。仪式分两部分：一部分为交换戒指时的订婚礼；另一部分是新郎和新娘在戴婚礼冠时的结婚仪式。这些婚礼冠具有象征意义，意味着新婚夫妇像国王和王后一样在他们家的王国里主持家庭生活。婚礼的最后，新郎和新娘在一个小圈子里走动，共同迈出他们作为丈夫和妻子的第一步。

---

willingness *n.* 意愿
emblem *n.* 象征

betrothal *n.* 订婚
preside *v.* 主持

17

Making a Match: The Role of the Shadchan

Finding a *spouse* is a serious matter in most cultures. For Jewish people, this process is called a *shidduch*, or *matchmaking*. A good match brings together young people whose characters and talents *complement* each other. It also unites families that share many values.

During the thirteenth and fourteenth

做媒：职业媒人的角色

在大多数的文化中，寻找配偶是一件严肃的事情。对犹太人来说，这个过程被称作牵线，或者做媒。一个完美的搭配可以使两个年轻人的性格和天分得到互补。也可以组成家庭来分享许多价值观念。

在13世纪和14世纪期间，战争和宗教迫害瓦解了已确立的犹太社

---

spouse *n.* 配偶　　　　　　　　　　　shidduch *n.* 牵线
matchmaking *n.* 做媒　　　　　　　　complement *v.* 补充

centuries, wars and religious *persecution* broke up well-established Jewish communities and sent many families in search of new homes. It also became harder to make a shidduch for a son or daughter. During this time, the role of the shadchan, or matchmaker, evolved from that of respected advisor to paid professional.

The *shadchanim* traveled throughout Europe. They became very familiar with countless families, learned the details of their histories, and found out what made each one special. Such journeys were not without dangers, however. Robbers *lurked* along the way, and roads were often in poor repair.

Jewish law recognized that the shadchanim put their lives at risk

---

区，从而使许多家庭寻找新的住所。这也为儿子或女儿说媒增加了难度。在这期间，媒人或者介绍人，由受人尊敬的顾问发展成须付费的职业人员。

媒人环游整个欧洲。他们对无数的家庭非常熟悉，了解他们历史的细节，然后找出每个人的特别之处。尽管这样的旅行并不是没有危险的。强盗在路上埋伏，而且路况很差。

犹太法律意识到，媒人在完成独特的服务时将他们的生命置于危险

---

persecution *n.* 迫害
lurk *v.* 埋伏

shadchanim *n.* 媒人

while performing a unique service. When the bride or groom came from far away, the parents often had to pay the matchmaker a high fee. By the fifteenth century, there were clear *guidelines* about when, and how much, the shadchan should be paid. There were also other rules *concerning* unhappy matches as well as extremely successful ones.

之中。当新娘或新郎从很远的地方到来时，他们的父母经常要付给媒人很高的费用。直到15世纪，才有关于何时和应该支付给媒人多少钱的明确指南。还有其他的关于不幸福的配对和极其成功的结合的规定。

guideline *n.* 指南   concern *v.* 关于

18

The Changing Roles of American Women

Women's rights movements first began to emerge in the early 1800s. The *Industrial Revolution* was changing patterns of work and family life. The rural lifestyle, in which each family produced its own food and household goods, was fading. Freed from the need to labor at home, many middleclass women

美国女性的角色转换

女权运动最早开始出现于19世纪早期。工业革命改变了工作和家庭生活的方式。每个家庭自己供己食物和家居用品的乡村生活方式逐渐消失了。从必需的劳动中解放出来的许多中产阶级妇女把她们的

---

industrial *adj.* 工业的   revolution *n.* 革命

directed their energies toward social and religious *activism*.

Some women grew troubled by what they saw as their *inferior* social status. Some formed movements in support of property and voting rights for women and better education for girls. Their efforts improved women's social and legal standing somewhat. However, women who wanted to excel in the "man's world" faced an *uphill* battle. They usually had to start with family advantages or conquer huge *obstacles*.

Elizabeth Blackwell was the first woman to earn a degree as a medical doctor. The only school that would admit her did so as a fluke. The faculty at Geneva Medical College in New York turned the decision over to the all-male student body. Treating the request as a

---

精力用到社会和宗教行动主义中。

有些妇女开始不安起来，因为她们看到了自己低下的社会地位。有些运动支持妇女财产权、选举权以及让女童接受更好的教育的权利。这些努力在某种程度上改善了妇女的社会地位和法律地位。然而，妇女想要在男人的世界里出类拔萃，必须面对艰苦的斗争。她们经常不得不从家庭的优势开始，或者战胜巨大的困难。

伊丽莎白·布莱克威尔是第一个获得学位的女医师。唯一肯录取她的学校这么做是出于偶然。坐落于纽约的日内瓦医学院把决定权交给了全体

---

activism *n.* 行动主义
uphill *adj.* 艰难的

inferior *adj.* 低等的
obstacle *n.* 困难

joke, they voted to admit her. When she arrived, townspeople *gawked* at her. Her male classmates *giggled* and blushed during certain *sensitive anatomy* demonstrations. Even so, she graduated first in her class in 1849 and went on to have a long career in medicine.

Maria Mitchell, the first American to discover a comet, had strong support from her father, a Quaker. He believed that girls should have the same education as boys. He observed stars for the U.S. Coast Guard and trained Maria in astronomy. She became famous after her comet discovery. She was voted the first woman member of the American Academy of Arts and Sciences in 1848 and of the Association for the Advancement of Sciences in 1850. In 1865 she became professor of astronomy at Vassar College in New York.

男性学生。他们把申请当做了玩笑，投票决定接收她。当她到达时，镇上的居民都呆呆地盯着她。在一些敏感的解剖演示中，她的男同学们咯咯地笑，并感到很害羞。即使是这样，1849年她是班级里面第一个毕业的，并开始长期从事医疗事业。

第一个发现彗星的美国人玛利亚·米切尔从她父亲———一名教友派信徒——那里获得了强有力的支持。他认为女孩子必须像男孩子一样接受同等的教育。他为美国海岸警卫队观察星相，在天文学方面训练玛利亚。在她发现彗星后，她就变得有名气了。她分别于1848年和1850年被投票选

---

gawk *v.* 呆呆地看着
sensitive *adj.* 敏感的

giggle *v.* 咯咯地笑
anatomy *n.* 解剖学

Mary Ann Shadd Cary also had a *supportive* father. She was born into a free African American family in Delaware in 1823. Her father sent her to a Quaker boarding school in Pennsylvania. At that time, education was not open to African Americans in Delaware. Cary went on to become a teacher, newspaper publisher, and activist. She published the *Provincial Freeman*, using her *initials* on the *masthead* instead of her first name to *disguise* the fact that she was a woman. At the age of 60, she became one of the first American women to earn a law degree.

举为美国艺术科学院、进步科学协会第一位女性成员。1865年在纽约的瓦萨学院她成为了天文学教授。

　　玛丽·安·赛德·卡里也有一个支持她的父亲。1823年她出生于特拉华自由的非裔美国家庭。她的父亲把她送到宾夕法尼亚的一个教友派寄宿学校。那时，在特拉华教育不对非裔美国人开放。卡里先后成为了一名教师、报纸出版者和积极分子。她出版了《地方自由民》，在报刊的报头她用了姓名的首字母而不是她的名字来掩饰她事实上是名女性。60岁的时候，她成为了第一批获得法律学位的美国妇女之一。

supportive *adj.* 支持的　　　　　　　　　　initial *n.* 首字母
masthead *n.* 报刊杂志名称　　　　　　　　disguise *v.* 掩饰

19

Helen Keller's Activism

Helen Keller, beloved author and *humanitarian*, is best known, perhaps, for the story of her *extraordinary* childhood. Left blind and deaf after an illness at the age of 19 months, she became, as she described it, "a wild, *unruly* child." When Keller was six years old, however, her parents hired Anne Sullivan to

海伦·凯勒的行动主义

海伦·凯勒是深受爱戴的作家和人道主义者。也许，她是由于她不同寻常的童年故事而为人所知的。在她19个月大时，一场病导致她又盲又聋。就如她描述的那样，她变成了"一个粗野的没有规矩的小孩儿。"在凯勒6岁的时候，她的父母聘请了安妮·沙利文做她的老

humanitarian *n.* 人道主义者　　　　extraordinary *adj.* 特别的；不平常的
unruly *adj.* 不遵守规章的

be her teacher. By teaching Keller to *communicate* with sign language, Sullivan helped Keller escape from her dark, silent, *isolated* world.

By the time Keller graduated from Radcliffe College, she had become a social activist. She spoke out for the rights of women, workers, and *minorities*. She supported *strikers* and campaigned for women's right to vote. In 1909 she joined the Socialist Party and worked on behalf of such socialist causes as trade unions. Keller also worked to put an end to child labor. As a pacifist, she spoke out against U.S. involvement in World War I.

In the course of her work, Keller learned that blindness most often

---

师。通过教凯勒用手语沟通，沙利文帮助凯勒逃出了她那黑暗、沉默、孤独的世界。

凯勒从拉德克利夫学院毕业时，她已经成为了一个社会活动家。她为妇女、工人以及少数人的权利说话。她支持罢工者和妇女选举权利运动。1909年她加入社会党，为像工会那样的社会党事业而工作。凯勒也为废除使用童工而努力。作为一名和平主义者，她反对美国卷入第一次世界大战。

在她工作的过程中，凯勒了解到，因为工伤事故和危险的生活条件，

---

communicate *v.* 交流

minority *n.* 少数

isolated *adj.* 孤立的

striker *n.* 罢工者

struck the poor because it was often caused by work accidents and *hazardous* living conditions. She decided that her life's work was to be a *spokesperson* for the blind. She began to work with the American Foundation for the Blind in 1924 and served as its chief fund-raiser until her death in 1968, at the age of 87.

穷人更容易失明。她决定毕生都要做盲人的发言人。1924年她开始在盲人基金会工作。她于1968年去世，享年87岁。直到去世时她都是基金会的主要募捐者。

---

hazardous *adj.* 危险的   spokesperson *n.* 发言人

20

The Russians and the Aleuts

In the late 1700s, Russian explorers became the first Europeans to land on the group of islands that extend in an east-west *arc* from the Alaskan Peninsula. Today, these islands are known as the Aleutians. The Native peoples that the Russians *encountered* are the Aleuts. The islands' environment was rich, yet often harsh,

俄罗斯人和阿留申人

在18世纪末，俄罗斯探险家们成为最初登陆这个岛屿群的欧洲人。这些岛屿群是成东西向弧状自阿拉斯加半岛延伸过来的。今天，这些岛屿被称为阿留申群岛。俄罗斯人遇到的本土居民就是阿留申人。岛屿群上的环境资源很丰富，但是经常很严酷，并且岛屿群被海洋环

---

arc *n.* 弧 encounter *v.* 遇见

and centered around the sea. The lives of the people, who called themselves Unangan, were shaped and defined by their dependence on the seals, whales, and sea otters that abounded there. *Ironically* it was the Russians' shared interest in these sea *mammals* that destroyed the Unangan way of life.

At the time of the Russians' arrival, about 15 thousand Unangan made these islands their home. They lived in villages of various sizes. The larger villages were located close to salmon streams and were made up of large *communal* houses called ulaxes. Ulaxes, which were built partially underground, could be 200 feet long or longer. Unangan society was organized into social classes consisting of enslaved people, common folk, and *nobility*. Archaeological evidence

---

绕。自称为尤南干的居民依靠周围的海豹、鲸鱼和海獭生活。讽刺的是俄罗斯人对于海洋哺乳动物的利益分享毁掉了尤南干人的生活方式。

在俄罗斯人到达的时候，大约有15 000名尤南干人在这些岛屿上定居。他们居住于大小不一的村庄里。比较大的村庄离鲑鱼河很近，它们是由巨大的被称作优莱克斯的公共房子组成的。半地下的优莱克斯大约有200英尺长或者更长。尤南干社会阶级组成有奴隶、普通人和贵族。考古

---

ironically *adv.* 讽刺地
communal *adj.* 公用的

mammal *n.* 哺乳动物
nobility *n.* 贵族

suggests that this social structure had existed since about 1200.

The Unangan were skilled hunters of sea mammals. They *harpooned* their *quarry* from sturdy, flexible, kayak-like boats called iqats. An iqat had a frame made of shaped driftwood bound with sinew, bone, and baleen (whalebone). The frame was covered with sealskin and coated with *watertight* layers of seal oil. In search of their prey, hunters performed many *elaborate* rituals in preparation for each hunt.

Sea animals provided most of the products the Unangan needed to survive. Women sewed warm, waterproof garments of skin and seal gut. Seal meat was an important part of the Unangan's diet.

证据显示这个社会结构大约自1200年就开始存在了。

尤南干人是娴熟的海洋哺乳动物猎手。他们从坚固且柔韧的叫艾格茨的皮艇状的船上用鱼叉捕获猎物。艾格茨船的框架是由筋、骨头和鲸须捆在一起的成型的浮木组成的。框架被海豹皮覆盖，并涂上防水的海豹油。为了寻找猎物，每一次的狩猎准备，猎手都要进行许多复杂的仪式。

海洋动物提供了尤南干人生活所需的大多数产品。妇女缝制了暖和、防水的皮袍子。海豹肉是尤南干人饮食中的重要部分。他们也采集贝类、

---

harpoon *v.* 用鱼叉
watertight *adj.* 防水的

quarry *n.* 猎物
elaborate *adj.* 复杂的

They also gathered *shellfish*, sea grasses, and kelp, and they picked berries.

The Unangan's boat-handling and hunting skills left the Russians *awestruck*. Unable to master these skills themselves, the Russians forced Unangan hunters to hunt for them. When the Unangan resisted, the Russians, armed with *rifles* (which the Unangan lacked), killed these Native people. The Russians also *kidnapped* Unangan wives and children, returning them at the end of the hunting season—if at all. Unangan women and children became malnourished without the meat and skins they were used to. Within 50 years after the Russians' arrival, two-thirds or more of the Unangan population had died as a result of starvation, disease, and war.

海藻、褐藻，也采摘浆果。

尤南干人的造船和狩猎技术让俄罗斯人崇敬。俄罗斯人自己不能掌握这些技术，就强迫尤南干猎手为他们狩猎。当尤南干人拒绝时，俄罗斯人就用步枪（这是尤南干人没有的）杀害这些本土居民。俄罗斯人还绑架了尤南干人的妻子和孩子，在狩猎季节结束的时候才把他们送回来。没有他们习惯的兽肉和毛皮，尤南干的妇女和儿童变得营养不良。在俄罗斯人到来的五十年内，三分之二甚至更多的尤南干人死于饥饿、疾病和战争。

---

shellfish *n.* 水生贝壳类　　　　　awestruck *adj.* 崇敬的
rifle *n.* 步枪　　　　　　　　　kidnap *v.* 绑架

21

The Aleuts of the Pribilofs

At first contact between the Russians and the Unangan, the Pribilof Islands were *uninhabited*. Located about two hundred miles north of the Aleutian chain, they were known only in *legend* as the breeding grounds of the fur seal. In 1786 the Russians found this valuable source of furs for the European market. They *forcibly*

普里比洛夫群岛的阿留申人

在俄罗斯人第一次接触尤南干人时，普里比洛夫群岛是无人居住的。它位于阿留申山脉以北两百英里，仅仅是因为在传奇中它是海狗的繁殖地而闻名。在1786年，俄罗斯人为欧洲市场发现了这一值

---

uninhabited *adj.* 无人居住的   legend *n.* 传奇
forcibly *adv.* 强迫地

relocated Aleut hunters to the islands and put them to work killing seals.

The Aleuts began life on the Pribilofs as slave labor, but *eventually*, they gained the rights of Russian subjects. They were paid fair wages and were able to maintain their traditional culture and some self-rule. But in 1867, after the United States bought the Alaskan Territory, conditions worsened. The Aleuts lost their rights and became an *exploited* labor force. They harvested seals for *meager* wages, and the U.S. government took the profits from the sale of furs. This situation continued until the United States abandoned the trade in 1983. With this loss of their only source of income, the Aleuts suffered even

---

钱的毛皮资源。他们强迫阿留申猎人迁徙到岛上，并让他们捕杀海豹。

　　阿留申人在普里比洛夫群岛开始了奴隶般的生活，但最终，他们得到了俄罗斯国民的权利。他们得到合理的工资，能够保留传统的文化习俗并且可以在某些方面自治。但是在1867年，在美国买下阿拉斯加之后，情况就变糟了。阿留申人失去了他们的权利并且成为了受剥削的劳动力。他们为了微薄的工资而去猎捕海豹，而美国政府则从海豹毛皮的交易中获

---

eventually *adv.* 最终　　　　　　　　　　　　exploited *adj.* 被剥削的
meager *adj.* 微薄的

worse poverty. They received $20 million from the U.S. government and used the money to develop new sources of *livelihood*. Today the Pribilof Aleuts have successful halibut- and crab-fishing industries. They have also begun programs to reacquaint their young people with traditional ways and encourage *preservation* of the environment.

取利润。这种状况一直持续到1983年美国放弃这项贸易。失去了这唯一的收入来源后，阿留申人遭受了更贫穷的状况。他们得到来自美国政府两千万美元的资金，并且使用这笔钱去发展新的生存资源。今天普里比洛夫群岛的阿留申人成功地拥有了自己的大比目鱼产业和捕蟹产业。他们也开始了用传统方式培育年轻人的项目，并且鼓励环境保护。

---

livelihood *n.* 生活   preservation *n.* 保护

22

Map Projections

Of all types of maps available, a globe can show distances, areas, directions, and shapes most closely to the way they actually exist on Earth's surface. However, for practical purposes, *flat* maps present obvious advantages over globes. They can be *folded* up and stored or carried around easily. Because they can be drawn

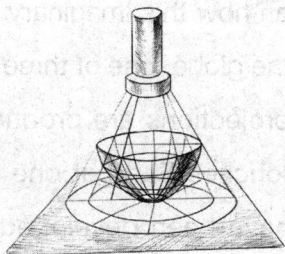

地图投影法

在各种类型的地图当中，地球仪能以最接近真实存在的地球表面的样子显示距离、地区、方向和形状。然而，出于实用目的，平面地图显然比地球仪更加有优势。它们可以折叠起来便于存放和携带。因为它们可以画出大比例尺寸，它们就可以展示小的细节，而这对于地球仪来说是做不到的。

---

flat *adj.* 平面的   fold *v.* 折叠

to large scales, which would not be practical for globes, they can show small details.

Cartographers have developed various *mathematical* means, called *projections*, of translating images of Earth's curved surface into a flat form.

Projections are *calculated* mathematically, but they work something like this: Imagine a light inside a globe projecting an image of Earth's surface onto a piece of paper wrapped around the globe. Depending on how this imaginary piece of paper touches or is wrapped around the globe, one of three basic types of map projections results. Planar projections are produced as though the imaginary piece of paper touches Earth at one point. (The gnomonic projection, believed to have been developed by the Greek mathematician Thales in the

---

　　地图制作者们开发了各种叫做投影法的数学方式，来把地球弯曲的表面转化成平面形式。

　　投影按数学方式计算，但他们是这样做的：想象地球内部的一束光投射在地球表面，映射在包裹地球表面的一张纸上。三种基本的投影法的结果，取决于这张想象的纸怎样接触或包裹着地球。平面投影法假设这张纸接触地球的一个点。（球心投影，被认为是希腊数学家泰利斯在公元前500年提出的，它是一种平面投影法。）圆锥投影法是假设这张纸折成圆

---

cartographer *n.* 地图制作者；制图师　　　　　mathematical *adj.* 数学的
projection *n.* 投影法　　　　　　　　　　　　calculate *v.* 计算

500s B.C., is a planar projection.) *Conical* projections are produced as though the paper were formed into a cone and perched on the globe. *Cylindrical* map projections are drawn as if the paper were wrapped around the globe to form a cylinder.

Although flat maps are of much practical use, their usefulness comes at a price—*distortion*. In other words, a map can show true distances, true directions, true areas, or true shapes, but never all four. *Conformal* maps, for example, show true shapes, but sizes are distorted. Equal-area projections show the correct sizes of areas in relation to one another, but shapes are distorted. Distortions result from the shrinking, slicing, and stretching that must occur when a spherical Earth is shown on a flat surface. Map users choose the map projection that produces the least distortion in the feature that

---

锥体状置于地球的顶端。圆柱投影法是假设这张纸包裹在地球表面形成一个圆柱体。

尽管平面地图有许多实际用途，但这些用处要以失真为代价。也就是说，一个地图能展示真实的距离，真实的方向，真实的地区或者是真实的形状，但是决不能将这四个方面全部真实地展示出来。例如，正形地图能展示真实的形状，但是大小会失真。等积投影能展示每一个地区正确的大小，但是形状会失真。失真是由于收缩、切断、延伸导致的，然而这些是

---

conical *adj.* 圆锥形的   cylindrical *adj.* 圆柱的
distortion *n.* 失真   conformal *adj.* 正形投影的；等角的

is most important for their specific purpose. Planar projections are useful for mapping polar areas. Because of its shape and size, the United States can be mapped with fair *accuracy* by using a conical projection. The Robinson projection falls into no single *category* of projections. It is, in effect, a *compromise* projection because it has some distortion in each major feature, but it gives a picture of Earth's land masses that is close to reality. This quality makes it a popular map for use in teaching *geography*.

在球形的地球转化成平面时必然发生的。地图使用者可以选择在他们所需要的方面尽可能不失真。平面投影法对于极地地区有很大帮助。由于形状和大小，美国可以用圆锥投影法精确地绘制出来。罗宾逊透射法没有单一的投射方法。也就是，实际上，折中的方法因为它在每一主要的方面都有失真的地方，但是它又展示了最接近实际情况的地球表面。这一特点使它成为地理教学中广泛使用的一种地图。

accuracy *n.* 精确   category *n.* 类型
compromise *adj.* 折中的   geography *n.* 地理学

23

Mercator If by Sea

In the late 1400s, increasingly fast, sturdy ships made long-distance voyages possible for European seafarers. The maps available at that time, however, were *inadequate* for plotting courses over long distances. Maps were drawn as if places were connected by curved lines. This was done to *replicate* the way places

如果在海上航行使用墨卡托投影

在15世纪晚期，坚固的轮船使欧洲船员长途航海变成可能，航海业快速发展。然而，那时可用的地图在长途路线的设计上并不充分。绘制的地图上的地点像是被曲线连接而成的。这种方式被用于复制地球表面上的地方。结果航海员不得不通过曲线来计算航行路线。海员依

---

inadequate *adj.* 不充足的   replicate *v.* 复制

are situated on Earth's surface. As a result, sailors had to calculate courses by using curved lines. Sailors who plotted a straight-line course toward their *destination* would end up somewhere else because of distortion. This situation can be compared to what happens when an arrow is aimed at a target far away. The archer cannot aim directly at the target because gravity causes the arrow's path to curve downward. The archer must aim above the target in order to hit it. The greater the distance, the greater the distortion.

Flemish cartographer Gerardus Mercator solved this problem in 1569. He devised a cylindrical map in which the *curvature* of directional lines is mathematically *eliminated*. There is no distortion of

照直线航向目的地通常会因为曲线的问题而到达别的地方。这种情况就好比是射向远处目标的箭。弓箭手不能直接瞄准目标,因为重力会使箭的路径弯曲向下。弓箭手为了击中它就必须瞄准目标以上。距离越远,曲线就越大。

　　1569年佛兰德人的制图师吉哈德斯·墨卡托解决了这一问题。他设计了一个圆柱形的地图,方向线的曲率在数学上是可以消除的。而在墨卡托地图上没有方向的弯曲。地图上任何地方的一条直线都可以显示真实的

destination *n.* 目的地　　　　　　　　　　　curvature *n.* 曲率
eliminate *v.* 消除

direction on a Mercator map. A straight line drawn anywhere on the map shows true direction. Using this map, sailors could calculate their courses across the ocean in straight lines instead of *curves*. Even though distance and area is distorted near the polar regions, these distortions were not important to sailors using the map.

方向。用这个地图，航海员可以用直线而非曲线来计算他们的航海路线。即使距离和区域扭曲到了极地附近，这些变形也不会对使用地图的船员那么重要。

curve *n.* 曲线

24

The Electoral College

In the United States, most leaders are chosen by direct votes during political elections. In a direct vote, people cast ballots for the *candidates* of their choice. The winners are those who receive the most votes. The president, however is not elected by a direct vote of the people. The winner is decided through a *majority* vote in

总统选举团

在美国，大多数领导人都是在政治选举中通过直接选票被选举出来的。在直接选举中，人们为他们选举的候选人投票，胜利者就是那些获得票数最多的人。然而，总统不是被人民群众直接推选出来

---

candidate *n.* 候选人   majority *n.* 大部分；大多数

the Electoral College.

The Electoral College system was created by the U.S. Constitution. In this system, voters cast ballots for both *electors* and a presidential candidate. Then the electors choose the president. In 48 of the 50 states, the electors have to vote for the candidate who receives the most votes in that state. Except in Maine and Nebraska, it is largely a "winner takes all" system. Many have argued, in fact, that this process ignores the ballots cast by many voters.

The number of electors in each state equals the number of that state's members of Congress. No state has fewer than three electors, because each state has at least two *senators* and one *representative*. States with larger *populations* have more electors

---

的。获胜者是由总统选举团中占大多数的选票决定的。

总统选举团制度是由美国宪法制定的。在这个制度中，投票者为选举人和总统候选人投票。然后选举人再选择总统。在50个州中的48个州里，选举人不得不为得到最多选票的候选人投票。除了缅因州和内布拉斯加州，它们是"赢家通吃"的制度。事实上许多人都在争论，这个过程忽视了许多选举人所投的选票。

在每个州中选举人的数量相当于那个州的国会成员的数量。没有一个州能少于3名选举人，因为每个州有至少2名参议员和1名代表。拥有大量

---

elector *n.* 选举人　　　　　　　　　　senator *n.* 参议员
representative *n.* 代表　　　　　　　　population *n.* 人口

than those with fewer *residents*. In the year 2000, California, as the most populous state, had the most electors: 54. Seven states and the District of Columbia had just three electors. The system was designed to *boost* the voting power of smaller states. In 2000, for instance, there were about two and a half million *eligible* voters in five of the smallest states and the District of Columbia. Together they controlled 18 *electoral* votes. Michigan, by contrast, has more than seven million voting-age residents. It, too, controlled 18 electoral votes.

The Electoral College has one curious feature. It is possible for the candidate who wins the majority of the popular vote to lose the race in the Electoral College. How can this be? It is a matter of math

---

人口的州比那些人口少的州有更多的选举人。在2000年，加利福尼亚作为人口最多的州，有最多的选举人，共54名。7个州和哥伦比亚地区仅仅有3名选举人。这种制度的设计用来增强小州的选举力量。例如，在2000年，在最小的5个州和哥伦比亚地区有250万选民。加在一起他们控制18张选票。相反，美国密歇根州有700多万选民，同样也控制着18张选票。

　　总统选举团有个不寻常的的特征。对于赢得大多数候选票的候选人来说，在总统选举团中失利也是很有可能的。这是怎么回事呢？这是一个数

---

resident *n.* 居民　　　　　　　　　　　　boost *v.* 增强
eligible *adj.* 合格的　　　　　　　　　　electoral *adj.* 选举的

and the "winner takes all" rule—*especially* important in a year when three or more candidates are running for president. The successful candidate in a state with less than half the popular vote can still control all of its electoral votes. The losing candidate can win most of the popular vote *nationwide* but lose in enough big states to lose the electoral vote.

Such was the case, for instance, in 1888 when Grover Cleveland lost to Benjamin Harrison and in 2000 when George W. Bush defeated Al Gore.

学问题，还有"赢家通吃"的原则，这在3名或者更多的候选者竞选总统的年份里尤为重要。在一个州中拥有少于半数直接选票的成功候选人，仍然能够掌控所有总统选举团所投的票。失败的候选人可以赢得全国范围的直接选票，但会因在大州中失败而失去总统选举团所投的票。

情况就是这样，例如，在1888年格罗弗·克利夫兰败给本杰明·哈里森，还有在2000年乔治·W·布什打败了阿尔·戈尔。

---

especially *adv.* 尤其

nationwide *adv.* 全国范围

25

Andrew Jackson and the Electoral System

The quirks of the Electoral College system have sometimes cast a cloud over election results. In 1824, for instance, four men *vied* for the office of president. Andrew Jackson won the largest *share* of both the popular and electoral votes. He did not, however, get a majority of either. Election rules required a decision from the

安德鲁·杰克逊和选举制度

总统选举团制度的突变有时会给选举结果蒙上一层阴影。例如在1824年，四个人竞选总统。安德鲁·杰克逊赢得了直接选票和总统选举团投票的最大份额。然而，他没有得到任何一种选票中的多数票。当时选举制度需要美国众议院的决定。结果出来后，约翰·昆西·亚

---

vie *v.* 竞争   share *n.* 份额

House of Representatives. After deals were struck, John Quincy Adams was the choice for president in 13 out of the 24 states.

Many people were *outraged*. Jackson spent the next four years on the campaign trail. After four years, changes in many state laws worked to his benefit. More people had become eligible to vote. The choice of electors was taken away from most state *legislatures* and given to the voters. A number of local offices were changed from appointed ones to elected ones. A surge in voter fervor greatly increased turnout.

Jackson beat Adams in the 1828 election. He took 56 percent of

---

当斯获得24个州中的13个州的支持而当选总统。

很多人表示非常气愤。杰克逊接下来花了四年时间致力于总统竞选。四年之后，很多州法律的改变使他受益。更多的人有了选举权。选举人的选择从大多数州的立法机关剥除，而把这个机会给了普通选民。很多当地的政府机关从任命制改为选举制。选民的热情使投票人数急剧上升。

在1828年的总统选举中，杰克逊打败了亚当斯。他赢得了56%的直接

---

outraged *adj.* 气愤的   legislature *n.* 立法机构

the popular vote and two-thirds of the votes in the Electoral College. In 1832 Jackson was reelected by an even larger electoral *margin*.

Success in the Electoral College did not make Jackson like the system. As president he tried without success to eliminate the Electoral College system and change the way the president is chosen.

选票以及三分之二的总统选举团选票。1832年杰克逊以更大的优势继任美国总统。

在总统选举团中的成功并没有使杰克逊喜欢这个制度。作为总统，他试图废除总统选举团制度，改变选择总统的方式，但是没有成功。

---

margin *n.* 差距

26

A Navel Journey

The sweet, juicy orange has come a long way from its original *birthplace*. The ancient orange was a bitter fruit. It probably became established in Southeast Asia about 20 million years ago. People began to develop the modern, or sweet, orange in Asia 5,000 to 6,000 years ago. Through the ages, careful *tending* changed

脐橙之旅

甜多汁的橙子从它的原始发源地远道而来。古代的橙子是一种有点苦的水果。大约在2000万年前橙子在东南亚开始种植。5000到6000年以前在亚洲，人们开始培育现代甜橙。随着时间的流逝，人们精心的照顾使这种野生的橙子转变成今天受人们喜爱的甘甜可口的橙子。学者们不确定人们是在什么地方第一次种植橙子来吃的。尽管如此，

---

birthplace *n.* 发源地

tend *v.* 照顾

this wild form into the tasty treat enjoyed today. *Scholars* are unsure where people first grew oranges for eating. However, China, India, *Bhutan*, *Malaysia*, and *Burma* are strong possibilities.

From Asia sweet oranges spread to North Africa and then to Spain and Portugal. European explorers planted orange trees in warm, humid parts of North and South America about 1500. Growers began raising oranges in Brazil about 1530. After many years, a sweet, thick-skinned, seedless orange grew naturally. What set this orange apart was a small lesser fruit, or navel, rooted in the top. This orange variety, called the Bahia orange, was discovered about 1800.

About 1870, a missionary in Brazil, impressed with the Bahia orange, sent some trees to the U.S. Department of Agriculture (USDA) in Washington, D.C. A couple named Eliza and Luther

中国、印度、不丹、马来西亚和缅甸有最大的可能性。

甜橙子从亚洲先传到北非，然后到西班牙和葡萄牙。大约在1500年，欧洲探险家在温暖潮湿的北美和南美部分地区种植橙子树。大约在1530年，巴西的种植者开始种植橙子。很多年之后，甘甜、厚皮、无籽的橙子自然地生长起来了。使这种橙子得到区分的是一种较小的水果或者叫脐橙，它的根长在顶部。这种橙子的品种被称作巴伊亚橙，它大约是在1800年被发现的。

大约在1870年，一名对巴伊亚橙子印象深刻的巴西传教士把一些橙树送到位于华盛顿的美国农业部。一对叫伊莱扎和卢瑟·蒂贝茨的夫妻，

scholar *n.* 学者   Bhutan *n.* 不丹
Malaysia *n.* 马来西亚   Burma *n.* 缅甸

Tibbets, who had just moved to Riverside, California, wrote to the USDA for information on the kind of trees they should plant at their new home. The USDA was eager to learn whether the Bahia oranges were suited to California's climate, so it sent the Tibbetses three trees in 1873. People began to talk about the Tibbetses' delicious fruit, which became known as the Washington *navel*. The Tibbetses' oranges won awards for their *outstanding* flavor. Soon the Tibbetses were selling starter *buds* from their trees for five dollars each.

The navels thrived in the *semidesert* climate of Riverside. However, the amount of rain that fell was often short of the trees' needs. In 1885 Matthew Gage gave the region's orange crops a big boost when he completed a 12-mile-long irrigation canal. The canal diverted water from the Santa Ana River to the groves of Riverside.

他们刚刚搬到加利福尼亚的河滨市。他们给美国农业部写信，要在他们的新家种植这种橙子树。美国农业部渴望知道这种巴伊亚橙子是否适宜加利福尼亚的气候，因此在1873年给了蒂贝茨一家三棵橙子树。人们开始谈论蒂贝茨家的美味可口的水果，这种水果被称为华盛顿脐橙。蒂贝茨家的橙子因其极佳的味道而赢得奖励。很快蒂贝茨一家开始卖从他们树上摘下的幼芽，一个五美元。

脐橙在河滨市的半沙漠气候地区生长得很茂盛。但是，这儿的降水量总是不能达到橙树的需要。在1885年，当马修·盖奇完成了一个12英里长的灌溉水渠的时候，这个区域的橙子收成得到了很大的提高。这个水渠

---

navel *n.* 脐橙
bud *n.* 芽

outstanding *adj.* 杰出的
semidesert *adj.* 半沙漠的

About the turn of the century, word that fortunes could be made by growing and selling oranges began to spread. By 1910 California boasted about one hundred thousand acres of *groves propagated* from the Tibbetses' trees, which still stand in what is now downtown Riverside. Protected by wrought iron fences and named a California state historical *landmark*, they are a permanent *tribute* to the importance of the orange in California.

把圣安娜河的河水引到了河滨市的果园。

在20世纪初，可以通过种植和售卖橙子创造财富的消息开始传播开来。到1910年加利福尼亚因从蒂贝茨家的橙子树上培植出十万英亩的橙树林而自豪。蒂贝茨家的橙子树一直坐落在河滨市的市中心。它们被精心制作的铁篱笆保护着并且被指定为加利福尼亚州的一个历史性地标。在加利福尼亚，它们对于橙子的重要性作了永久的贡献。

grove *n.* 小树林	**propagate** *v.* 培植；繁殖
landmark *n.* 地标；里程碑	**tribute** *n.* 贡献

27

Hazardous Harvests

California produces about four-fifths of the United States' table oranges, or oranges meant for eating. Most jobs related to the industry are done by Hispanic farm workers. They prune trees, apply *pesticides* and *fertilizers*, and pick the oranges by hand. In the fields, the workers pack the fruit in 50-pound boxes. At the

危险的收获

加利福尼亚生产的橙子大约占到美国餐桌上的或者说用来吃的橙子的五分之四。大多数与这个产业相关的工作都是由西班牙裔的农场工人完成的。他们修剪果树,喷洒农药和施肥,并且亲手采摘橙子。在果园里,工人们把水果装进50磅重的箱子里。在加工厂里,其他的

pesticide *n.* 农药　　　　　　　　　　fertilizer *n.* 化肥

packinghouses, other workers inspect, sort, and pack the oranges in shipping cartons.

The jobs provide scant income, little security, and major risks. The workers earn about six to eight dollars an hour, and few receive medical *coverage*. They sometimes climb ladders 18 to 20 feet high to reach the tops of trees. Falls are not uncommon. Because oranges are *vulnerable* to pests such as insects and worms, pesticides are applied. Orange production is second only to grape production in the rate of pesticide poisonings of workers. Although there are mandates in California to protect workers, laborers may be affected while applying the pesticides and while harvesting and packing the

---

工人检查、分类，然后把橙子装进装运箱里。

这种工作收入微薄，安全性很小，存在许多危险。工人们每小时赚6到8美元，而且几乎没人能得到医疗保险。他们有时爬到18到20英尺高的梯子上以便够到果树的顶端。从梯子上跌落下来并不稀奇。因为橙子易受到像昆虫和蠕虫等害虫的侵害，所以工人们喷洒农药。在工人遭受农药毒害的比率上，橙子产业位于第二位，是仅次于葡萄产业的。尽管在加利福尼亚有保护工人的要求，但工人们在喷洒农药、采摘或包装橙子时，仍然

---

packinghouse *n.* 加工厂   coverage *n.* 保险
vulnerable *adj.* 易受伤的

fruit.

Between 13,000 and 15,000 workers depend on the winter *citrus* harvest in the San Joaquin Valley. Some entire *communities* in the Central Valley also depend on the orange crop for their livelihood. In 1990 and 1998, freezes destroyed much of the citrus crop. Pickers and packinghouse workers had no work, and many families suffered great hardship.

可能会受到农药的影响。

在圣华金河山谷有13 000至15 000名工人依靠冬天的柑橘收获为生。在中央山谷也有一些群体要依靠橙子的收获为生。在1990年和1998年,上冻毁坏了许多柑橘作物。采摘工人和加工厂的工人失去了工作,许多家庭遭受了巨大的困难。

---

citrus *n.* 柑橘　　　　　　　　　　　　　community *n.* 群体;团体

28

The Birth of Credit and Debt

For as long as people have *desired* goods that they could not afford, there has been credit and debt. Records date back to the ancient city-states of Mesopotamia, in what is now *Iraq*. In the 3000s B.C., the practice of lending and borrowing worked much as it does today.

The discovery that money grows in

贷款和负债的由来

当人们没有支付他们渴望的物品的能力时，贷款和负债就应运而生。早在古代的城邦国家美索不达米亚，也就是现在的伊拉克，就有这方面的记载。在公元前3000年，借出和借入如同现在社会一样普遍。

人们发现，随着时间的推移货币会增值，这标志着现代贷款和债务业

---

desire *v.* 渴望

Iraq *n.* 伊拉克

value over time marked the beginning of modern credit-and-debt arrangements. Historians believe that ancient Mesopotamian *herders* first made this *connection*. They observed that when one *livestock* owner lent a herd to another, at least some of the animals would give birth during the time of the loan. To make up for that natural growth, the borrower would have to return more livestock than were originally lent. Sometime in the 2000s B.C., people learned to apply the same *principle* to other goods and to money. The concept of interest was born. When one person lent another person silver, for example, the lender would charge a certain percentage of the amount in interest over time. The interest rate was based in part on how much that

务的开始。历史学家认为这种关系的创始者是古代美索不达米亚的牧人。他们注意到，当畜牧人把他们的牲畜租给另一个人时，至少其中的一些牲畜会在租借期间产下幼畜。为弥补这一自然生产，借方就需要归还比原来要多的牲畜。在公元前2000年时，人们就学着把同样的原则用在其他商品和货币之中。利息的概念就产生了。比如说，当某人借给他人银子时，出借方将会按时间收总金额的百分之几作为利息。利息的比率就根据借方将银子用以经商或投资后银子增长的多少做参考，收取相应的一部分。

herder *n.* 牧人
livestock *n.* 家畜

connection *n.* 联系
principle *n.* 原则

silver would have increased in value had the lender used it to carry on business or make *investments*.

In the 1920s, the ruins of a financial district were found in the Mesopotamian city of Ur. Stone tablets show that lively lending and borrowing took place there in the 1800s and 1700s B.C. Merchants borrowed silver from one another to fund new businesses. Some individuals acted as banks. They paid *depositors* a small amount of interest. Then they used the money for their own ventures. They used it to set up a new business, to invest in the businesses of others, or to make loans at higher interest rates.

Such shifting of funds kept money flowing into new businesses

---

在20世纪20年代，在美索不达米亚的乌尔城发现了金融区的遗迹。石碑上显示着公元前19世纪和18世纪，这个地方借贷繁荣。商人从一方借银子来投资新生意。一些个人就承担了银行的角色。他们付给储户一小部分利息，然后他们再用这些钱来进行风险投资。他们可以开个新买卖，或者投资其他的生意，或者以较高的利率借贷给他人。

这种资金转移可以确保资金流入新的贸易中，促进了城市的财富和生产力。但是它也给为应急而去借款的穷人带来压力。出借方以高利率放出

---

investment *n.* 投资

depositor *n.* 储户

and added to the country's wealth and productivity, but it put great pressure on poor people who had to borrow money for *emergency* purposes. Lenders charged high interest rates for these short-term loans. Those who could not pay back their debts often had to sell themselves or family members into slavery. Sometimes, however, the tables would be turned on the lenders.

Rulers *occasionally* announced *kingdomwide forgiveness* of debt. Such announcements were a blessing for debtors, but they spelled financial ruin for lenders. Scholars believe that such a declaration, issued by King Rim-Sin in 1788 B.C., brought about a financial crash from which the city of Ur never recovered.

短期贷款，那些还不起贷款的人不得不将自己或家人卖为奴隶。然而有时形势会反过来不利于借方。

统治者偶尔会宣布全国范围的免除债务。这种公告对借贷者来说是一种恩赐，但对出借方就意味着经济损失。学者们认为在公元前1788年国王林辛的这一免债公告引发了一场金融危机，从而使乌尔城再没能从这次危机中走出来。

---

emergency *n.* 紧急情况
kingdomwide *adj.* 全国范围的

occasionally *adv.* 偶尔
forgiveness *n.* 免除

29

Using Credit Cards the Smart Way

Credit cards can make life easier or cause harm. It all depends on how they are used.

Because the terms of credit cards vary greatly, smart users know how they plan to use a card before they apply for one. A person who plans to use a credit card to finance purchases *generally* chooses

正确地使用信用卡

信用卡既可以使生活更加轻松也可以造成危害。这完全取决于如何使用它们。

由于信用卡的条件各不相同，所以明智的使用者在申请前就知道怎样计划好使用它。那些打算用它购物的人通常会选择利息低一些的信用卡。还有些人使用信用卡以避免携带现金。他们通常每月还清余额。在这种情

generally *adv.* 通常

a card with a low interest rate. Another may use a card to avoid carrying cash. He or she usually pays off the balance every month. In this case, a card with no *annual* fee and a grace period is best. The grace period is a period of days or weeks between the time of purchase and the time the payment is due, during which no interest is charged.

A *shrewd* user examines *statements* carefully, compares the balance to funds available, and pays off as much of the balance as possible. Many people get into financial trouble with credit cards because they do not realize how quickly finance charges can add up. If they pay only the minimum amount each month and continue to add to the debt, they can find themselves in serious financial difficulty. They can *recover* from the problem by not using their cards until they can pay off most or all of every balance.

况下，一张没有年费和还款期限的卡是最佳选择。还款期限就是在消费日和还款日之间的这段时间，在此期间内是没有利息的。

一个精明的使用者会仔细地阅读声明，比较可利用的资金余额，并且尽可能地还清欠款。很多人使用信用卡而陷入了财政困难，这是因为他们没有认识到财务费用可以迅速叠加。如果他们每个月只还最低还款额并且继续增加债务，他们就会发现自己身处严重的财务困境。他们可以通过停止使用信用卡直到还清大部分或者全部余欠的钱数来摆脱困境。

---

annual *adj.* 年度的
statement *n.* 说明

shrewd *adj.* 精明的
recover *v.* 恢复

30

Gandhi and Nehru: Shared Goals, Opposing Values

The two chief figures in India's struggle for *independence* from British rule, Mohandas K. Gandhi and Jawaharlal Nehru, liked and respected each other. Despite their shared goals, however, their *visions* of an independent India differed in several ways. In the end, neither man's hope for his country was fully realized.

甘地和尼赫鲁：共同的目标，相对的价值观

这两名为了印度独立，摆脱英国统治而进行斗争的主要人物，莫罕达斯·K·甘地和贾瓦哈拉尔·尼赫鲁，相互欣赏并且互相尊敬。尽管他们有共同的目标，然而他们对印度独立的视角在好几个方面却不同。最后，没有一个人对国家的希望是完全实现的。

---

independence *n.* 独立　　　　　　　　　　　　　　　　　　vision *n.* 视角

Gandhi gained leadership of the Quit-India movement with his method of social change called satyagraha, or "truth force". *Nonviolent resistance* to British rule, said Gandhi, was the right way to gain independence. Acts of violence would only be met with greater violence. Peaceful refusal to submit to injustice, on the other hand, would show the British that the Indians' cause was just. The power of nonviolence would lead the British to leave the country willingly.

Gandhi wanted India to become a nation in which *spirituality* was the highest good. Indian life would be focused on small villages. There, simple means of livelihood, such as farming and the spinning of cloth, would be *prevalent*. People would take care of their own and treat one another fairly. Without pressure to create wealth, they

---

甘地以他的社会变革方式取得了印度独立运动的领导权，他的社会变革方式是非暴力的消极抵抗和不合作主义，或者叫做"真理的力量"。甘地说，以非暴力方式抵抗英国统治是获得独立的正确方式。暴力行为只会遇到更大的暴力。从另一方面说，以和平的方式拒绝屈服于非正义，将向英国显示印度的事业是正义的。非暴力的力量会使英国人心甘情愿地离开这个国家。

甘地想要印度成为一个精神至上的国度。印度人的生活将集中在小村落里。在那里，简单的生活方式，例如农耕和织布将会盛行。人们会照顾他们自己并公平地对待彼此。没有去创造财富的压力，他们可以自由地在

---

nonviolent *adj.* 非暴力的　　　　　　　　**resistance** *n.* 抵抗
spirituality *n.* 精神　　　　　　　　　　**prevalent** *adj.* 盛行的

would be free to grow spiritually. To Gandhi it was vital that India avoid the ways of Western industrial society, which he believed were based on greed and robbed people of their *dignity*.

Inspired by Gandhi's leadership, Nehru quickly became one of his most loyal followers. Their partnership grew despite the fact that Nehru called Gandhi's vision for India "completely unreal". Nehru valued technology and wanted India to become a modern world power. He shared Gandhi's *hatred* of social injustice. However, his solution was not to reject the production of wealth but to ensure that the wealth was shared fairly among the entire population.

India achieved independence in 1947. Nehru became the country's first *prime minister*. Less than a year later, Gandhi was dead,

---

精神上成长。对甘地来说至关重要的是，印度要避免实行西方工业社会的方式，他坚信那种方式是以贪婪和抢夺人民的尊严为基础的。

受甘地领导能力的鼓舞，尼赫鲁很快成为他的一位最忠实的追随者。他们的关系甚好，尽管事实上尼赫鲁称甘地对印度的设想是"完全不真实的"。尼赫鲁重视技术，想要印度成为一个现代化的世界强国。他认同甘地对社会不公的仇恨。然而他的解决方式不是拒绝财富创造，而是确保财富在所有人中公平分配。

印度在1947年取得了独立。尼赫鲁成为了这个国家第一位总理。不到一年后，甘地被刺身亡。他的非暴力抵抗社会不公的遗产，鼓舞了未来

---

dignity *n.* 尊严
prime minister 总理；首相

hatred *n.* 痛恨

killed by an *assassin*. His legacy of nonviolent resistance to social injustice would inspire future leaders such as Martin Luther King Jr., in the United States. During his almost 20 years in office, Nehru was able to guide India to a powerful position on the world stage under a *democratic*, *parliamentary* system of government. However, Nehru met with many social and political obstacles to his economic programs. As a result, many of the problems that both he and Gandhi had believed could be solved by independence—poverty, hunger, and disease—remained.

的像美国的马丁·路德·金这样的领导人。在他执政的近20年里，尼赫鲁能够在民主、议会的政府制度下，引导印度在世界舞台上取得强势地位。然而尼赫鲁在他的经济项目上却遇到了很多社会和政治上的障碍。因此，大多数尼赫鲁和甘地都坚信可以通过独立解决的问题——如贫穷、饥饿和疾病还依然存在。

---

assassin *n.* 刺客　　　　　　　　　　　　democratic *adj.* 民主的
parliamentary *adj.* 议会的

31

Celebrating Independence

Throughout history, many countries gained their freedom only after long, hard, and often bloody struggles against a foreign power. For this reason, nations around the world often mark the *anniversary* of their independence with rousing celebrations that may include *parades*, fireworks displays, flag flying, and

庆祝独立日

纵观历史，许多国家都是经过漫长、艰苦以及血淋淋地反抗外国强权的斗争才获得自身的自由。正是因为如此，世界各国经常以活跃的庆祝活动来庆祝他们的独立周年纪念日，这些庆祝活动包括游

---

anniversary *n.* 周年纪念日   parade *n.* 游行

official holidays.

Countries often add to their celebrations *elements* that have special meaning. Mexico celebrates its independence day, September 16, with the battle cry "*Mexicanos, viva México!*" and the ringing of church bells. On this day in 1810, the Roman Catholic priest Miguel Costillo rang his *parish* bell to call the people to Mass. Then, crying these words, he urged them to fight for their freedom from Spain. Mexicans did not win their freedom until 1821, but they still mark this day as the beginning of the end for Spanish rule.

In India many people celebrate their independence day by flying kites. The soaring kites *represent* the freedom that they won when,

---

行、焰火表演、飞舞彩旗或法定假日。

各国经常会加入具有特殊意义的庆祝元素。墨西哥以呐喊口号"墨西哥公民,墨西哥万岁!"和教堂的钟声,来庆祝每年9月16日的独立日。1810年的这天,罗马天主教的教士米克尔·科斯蒂亚,敲响了他教区的钟来召集人们团结起来。然后喊着这些口号号召人们为摆脱西班牙获得自由而战。墨西哥直到1821年才赢得自由,但是他们仍然把这天作为结束西班牙统治的开始。

在印度,许多人通过放风筝的方式来庆祝独立日。这些高飞的风筝象

---

element *n.* 元素   parish *n.* 教区
represent *v.* 象征

on August 15, 1947, the British gave up rule of India. *Finland*, in contrast, remembers its struggle for freedom with a more *solemn* rite. Each December 6, the day in 1917 on which Finland declared its independence from Russia, Finlanders attend formal dances, and many display two candles in their windows to pay tribute to those who fought during World War II.

征着他们赢得的自由，也就是在1947年8月15日，英国放弃印度统治权。芬兰却恰恰相反，他们用更加隆重的仪式纪念为自由所做的斗争。1917年12月6日，芬兰宣布摆脱俄罗斯而独立。每年的12月6日这天，芬兰人民参加正式的舞会，许多人在窗口摆放两根蜡烛，以此向在第二次世界大战中参加战斗的人致敬。

Finland *n.* 芬兰   solemn *adj.* 隆重的；庄严的

32

Sputnik Sparks the Space Race

In 1957 the Soviet Union launched the first *artificial* satellite into space. Its name was Sputnik 1, from the Russian word for satellite. Not much bigger than a basketball, Sputnik weighed less than 200 pounds. As it *orbited* Earth, it sent back radio signals that sounded like a cricket's chirps.

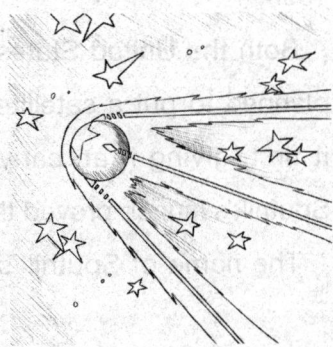

"斯普特尼克" 引发了太空竞赛

在1957年，前苏联发射了第一颗人造卫星，并将其送入太空。它的名字是斯普特尼克1号，斯普特尼克是俄语单词，意思是卫星。斯普特尼克没有篮球大，重不到200磅。当它绕地球轨道而行时，它就发回无线电信号，无线电信号听起来像蟋蟀的唧唧声。

---

artificial *adj.* 人造的   orbit *v.* 环绕轨道运行

At the time of Sputnik's launch, the United States and Soviet Union were engaged in the Cold War, which began after World War II ended. The Soviet Union had taken control of much of Eastern Europe. It became a *superpower* that competed with the United States. Each nation built up a supply of arms to defend itself from the other. The two nations also competed in space. The Cold War ended when the *Charter of Paris for a New Europe* was signed in 1990.

Both the United States and the Soviet Union had said that they planned to put a satellite into orbit in 1957. The Soviet Union did it first, giving it an early lead in the space race. It claimed that Sputnik's launch proved the *superiority* of *communism* over *capitalism*.

The name of Sputnik's builder was kept a secret until after his

---

在斯普特尼克发射时期，美国和前苏联正陷入冷战时期，这从第二次世界大战结束之后就开始了。前苏联已经控制了东欧的大部分地区。它已成为可与美国竞争的超级大国。每个国家都建立了武器供应来保卫自己。两个大国的竞争也进行到了太空。1990年"新欧洲巴黎宪章"签署之后冷战才结束。

在1957年，美国和前苏联双双表示他们计划把卫星送入轨道。前苏联第一个做到，占据了太空竞赛的早期领先地位。它声称斯普特尼克的发射证明共产主义优于资本主义。

斯普特尼克的建造者的名字一直被保密，直到1966年他死后才公

---

superpower *n.* 超级大国

communism *n.* 共产主义

superiority *n.* 优越性

capitalism *n.* 资本主义

MCGRAW-HILL

death in 1966. He was known only as its "chief designer". Sergei Pavlovich Korolev was one of many *aerospace* engineers *imprisoned* from 1937 to 1938 by Soviet premier Josef Stalin. He was released in 1938 to help develop weapons.

Korolev's dream was to build a rocket that could put a person on the moon; but the Soviet government had little interest in space *exploration*. Therefore, Korolev proposed that they launch a satellite to test the working of instruments in space. He pointed out that the satellite could also be used to collect *military* information about the United States.

Korolev's team began working on a satellite called Object D. They planned to fill it with equipment to study the atmosphere, Earth's magnetic fields, and the Sun. Then Korolev learned that the United

---

开。他仅被认为是斯普特尼克的"首席设计师"。谢尔盖·帕夫洛维奇·科罗廖夫是在1937年到1938年期间被前苏联领袖约瑟夫·斯大林囚禁的许多航天工程师中的一员。他于1938年被释放以帮助发展核武器。

科罗廖夫的梦想是建造一个火箭，可以把人送上月球；但前苏联政府对太空探索的兴趣不大。因此科罗廖夫建议他们发射一枚人造卫星，来测试太空中的仪器的工作。他指出卫星也可以用来收集关于美国的军事信息。

科罗廖夫的团队开始研究叫做"目标D"的卫星。他们计划增补设备，以研究大气、地球磁场以及太阳。后来科罗廖夫得知美国在做三级导

---

aerospace *adj.* 航天的

exploration *n.* 探索

imprison *v.* 监禁

military *adj.* 军事的

States was testing a three-stage *missile*. His team decided to build a smaller, simpler satellite. Ten months later, they sent Sputnik into orbit.

The United States won the race to land a person on the moon, but Sputnik's legacy endures. Its technology is now shared by the United States and Russia, partners in building the International Space Station. Other advances inspired by Sputnik include heart *monitors*, *microelectronics* used in computers, and the computer network that has become the Internet.

弹的测试。于是他的团队决定建一个更小、更简单的卫星。十个月后，他们将人造卫星送入运行轨道。

美国通过人类登月而赢得了这场比赛，但斯普特尼克的遗产仍将长存。现在它的技术被美国和俄罗斯共享，共同致力于建设国际空间站。受斯普特尼克影响的其他科技发展包括心脏监测仪、用于计算机中的微电子学，以及成为互联网的计算机网络。

---

missile *n.* 导弹　　　　　　　　　　　　　monitor *n.* 监测仪
microelectronics *n.* 微电子学

33

The "Sputnik Effect"

The *launch* of Sputnik in 1957 changed the way Americans learn science. Up to that time, the United States had been thought to have the best technology in the world. However, Sputnik showed that the Soviet Union was winning the space race. The satellite's orbit around the world also spread fears. People were worried that the

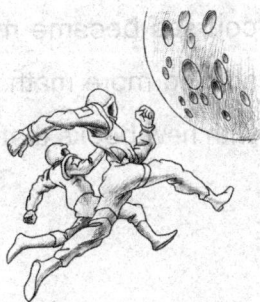

"斯普特尼克效应"

1957年"斯普特尼克"的发射改变了美国人学习科学的方式。在那之前，美国人一直被认为拥有全世界最先进的科技。然而，"斯普特尼克"展示了前苏联在太空竞赛的胜利。卫

---

launch *n.* 发射

Soviets could direct *atomic* bombs from space.

The United States quickly formed the National Aeronautics and Space Administration (NASA). However, more scientists and engineers were needed to win the space race. Science education was now *paramount* in the nation's defense.

The National Defense Education Act, passed in 1958, funded loans for students who were training for careers in science. High school students were required to take more science classes. The courses became more challenging. Even grade school students studied more math and science. *Outdated* textbooks were replaced with new books that covered more current theories.

星轨道围绕着世界也传播着恐惧。人们担心前苏联会从太空控制原子弹。

　　美国迅速组成了美国国家航空航天局（美国宇航局）。然而，这需要更多的科学家和工程师来赢得这场太空竞赛。在国家的防御上科学教育现在是最重要的。

　　在1958年国防教育法案被通过，给那些在科学事业上接受培训的学生们提供贷款。高中的学生被要求修习更多的科学课程。课程变得更有挑战性。甚至小学生也学习了更多的数学和科学。过时的课本被新书取代，这些新书涵盖了更多当今的理论。

atomic *adj.* 原子的　　　　　　　　　　　　paramount *adj.* 首要的
outdated *adj.* 过时的

Reformers also made changes in the way science was taught. Teachers began to stress *principles* instead of isolated facts. Hands-on activities gave students a chance to think like scientists. The new focus on "hard" science, however, meant that students spent less time exploring ways that science affects people's lives and their beliefs about scientific facts.

改革者也在教授科学的方法上做了改变。教师开始着重原理而不是孤立的事实。亲身实践的活动给了学生们像科学家们一样思考的机会。然而，关注"硬"科学这个新焦点意味着，在探索科学对人们生活影响的方式以及他们关于科学事实的信仰上，学生们花费的时间要少得多。

---

reformer *n.* 改革者　　　　　　　　　　　　　principle *n.* 原理

34

Japan's Unruly Geography

Japan, an island country in the northern Pacific Ocean, is located in the *midst* of three of Earth's tectonic plates. These are huge pieces of Earth's crust that "float" on the *partially* fluid hot rock in Earth's mantle layer. Two of these plates, the Pacific Plate and the Philippine Plate, are moving toward the third, the Eurasian

日本难以控制的地理活动

日本是太平洋北部的一个岛国，位于三个地球的构造板块当中。这三个地球板块是巨大的地壳，"漂浮"在地球地幔层部分的流动的热岩上。其中的两个板块，太平洋板块和菲律宾板块，正在向第三板块欧亚板块移动，并陷入它的下面。地震和火山都是与板块边界有关的

midst *n.* 中间　　　　　　　　　　　　　　partially *adv.* 部分地

Plate, and plunging beneath it. Both earthquakes and volcanoes are features *associated* with plate *boundaries*. Japan experiences about 15 hundred earthquakes every year and has at least 60 active volcanoes.

On September 1, 1923, the Great Kanto Earthquake struck the Tokyo area. It is estimated that the main quake lasted up to 10 minutes, with two and a half hours of constant trembling. One witness described a "*sickening* sway" and "*vicious* grinding of timbers". The quake struck about noon, when many people were cooking lunch over coal stoves. Fires broke out throughout the quake area. Flames quickly consumed Yokohama and burned for two days. From the first shaking on September 1 until the activity died down on September 6, more than 800 smaller quakes—called

---

特征。日本每年大约经历1500次地震并有至少60座活火山活动。

1923年9月1日，大关东地震袭击东京地区。据估计，这次主震持续长达10分钟，伴随两个半小时不断的震动。一位目击者描述这是"令人厌恶的摇摆"、"剧烈地在磨碎木料"。这次地震差不多发生在中午，当时许多人正在用煤火炉做饭。火灾在整个地震区爆发。大火很快烧毁了横滨，持续燃烧了两天。从9月1日第一次震动到9月6日平息下来，发生了

---

associate *v.* 联系   boundary *n.* 边界
sickening *adj.* 令人厌恶的   vicious *adj.* 剧烈的；严重的

aftershocks—occurred. In the end, most of Yokohama and one-third of Tokyo were destroyed, and more than 142 thousand people were dead.

The Great Hanshin Earthquake struck near Kobe on January 17, 1995. This quake caused almost 5,300 deaths and destroyed or seriously damaged about 241 thousand houses. As in the case of the Kanto earthquake, many of the deaths were a result of fires, but falling *debris* also took its *toll*. Traditional Japanese houses are made of wood frames topped with heavy clay-and-tile roofs. These buildings *withstand* fierce typhoons but not the shaking that occurs during strong earthquakes.

Between 1991 and 1995, the Unzen volcano erupted often. Heavy rains loosened debris on the slopes. This caused landslides.

800多次被称为余震的小震。最后，横滨市大部分和东京三分之一地区被毁，有142 000多人死亡。

1995年1月17日阪神大地震袭击神户附近地区。这次地震造成几乎5 300人死亡，严重摧毁了大约241 000座房屋。和在关东地震中一样，许多死亡是由火灾造成的，但掉落的碎片也造成了损失和伤亡。传统的日本房屋是木质结构，上面是沉重的黏土瓦片房顶。这些建筑能够承受猛烈的台风，但不能承受强烈地震中发生的震动。

从1991年到1995年，云仙火山经常喷发。大雨松动了山坡上的碎

---

aftershock *n.* 余震   debris *n.* 碎片
toll *n.* 损失   withstand *v.* 承受

Hundreds of houses were destroyed, dozens of people died, and thousands had to leave.

Earthquakes, volcanoes, and *landslides* may cause harmful ocean waves called *tsunamis*. Tsunamis begin when Earth movements set ocean water into motion. In the open ocean, tsunamis are harmless and even *undetectable*. When they approach shallow water close to land, however, the water piles up, creating a wave between 30 and 100 feet high. An eruption of the Unzen volcano in 1792 caused a landslide and a tsunami that killed some 15 thousand people. *Disastrous* tsunamis also struck Japan in 1883, 1896, 1983, and 1993.

片。这导致了山体滑坡。数以百计的房屋被毁，几十人死亡，数千人被迫离开。

地震、火山、滑坡都会引起叫做海啸的破坏性的海浪。当地壳运动引起海水移动时，海啸就开始了。在外海，海啸不能造成危害，甚至无法察觉。然而当它们接近靠近陆地的浅水区域时，海水聚积起来，就能产生30到100英尺高的波浪。1792年云仙火山喷发引起滑坡和海啸，造成15 000人死亡。灾难性的海啸也在1883年、1896年、1983年和1993年袭击了日本。

---

landslide *n.* 滑坡
undetectable *adj.* 无法察觉的

tsunami *n.* 海啸
disastrous *adj.* 灾难性的

35

What Is an Archipelago?

Japan is one of Earth's major archipelagos, or large island groups. Others include Hawaii, the Galapagos Islands, and the islands of the South Pacific. Although the origins vary, the islands that make up archipelagos were all formed the same way.

Many archipelagos were formed by

什么是群岛?

日本是地球上主要的群岛之一，或者说它是较大的岛群。其他的群岛包括夏威夷、加拉帕戈斯群岛，和南太平洋岛。尽管起源不同，但组成群岛的岛屿都以同样的方式形成。

许多群岛是由海底火山形成的。当火山喷发时，岩浆变硬，岛就形成

---

archipelago n. 群岛

undersea volcanoes. When such volcanoes *erupt*, *lava* hardens and builds up. In due course, it rises above the surface to form an island. The volcanoes that formed Japan arose from the meeting of three tectonic plates. Ironically, the earthquakes, volcanoes, and tsunamis that *buffet* Japan are the *consequence* of the same forces.

The volcanoes that formed the Hawaiian group resulted from hot spots—stationary plumes of magma, a molten-rock mixture, that form near a heat source in Earth's mantle. As a plate floats over a hot spot, the magma rises through the crust. An island is formed, and volcanic activity slowly fades as the plate moves away. The Galapagos Islands, known for their unique wildlife, were also formed

---

了。在适当的时候，它露出水面形成岛屿。形成日本的火山是由三大构造板块相撞引起的。具有讽刺意味的是，地震、火山，以及猛烈冲击日本的海啸，是同一外力的结果。

形成夏威夷群岛的火山是由热区形成的，热区就是冲天的岩浆冷却后的区域。岩浆是融化的岩石混合物，它是在地幔热源附近形成的。作为一个漂浮在热点上的板块，岩浆通过地壳上升，岛屿就形成了，并且随着板块移开，火山活动慢慢消失。以其独特的野生动物闻名的加拉帕戈斯群

---

erupt *v.* 喷发　　　　　　　　　　　lava *n.* 熔岩
buffet *v.* 打击　　　　　　　　　　consequence *n.* 结果

in this manner.

Many of the islands that make up the South Pacific archipelagos are coral islands, which begin as *volcanic* islands. Coral reefs grow around the islands. Over time the islands sink, or the water rises. The original islands disappear, but the coral reefs continue to grow until only circular reefs, called *atolls*, remain.

岛，也是以这种方式形成的。

构成南太平洋群岛的岛屿中有很多是珊瑚岛，它们是从火山岛开始的。珊瑚礁生长在这个岛周围。随着时间流逝，岛屿沉没，或者海水上升。原始岛屿消失，但珊瑚礁继续生长，直到只有长成圆形的珊瑚礁——环礁留下来。

---

volcanic *adj.* 火山的   atoll *n.* 环礁

36

The Tension Between Free Enterprise and Government Regulation

The *expression* "robber barons" was first used by Matthew Josephson, a social *critic*. It referred to some wealthy businessmen who made their fortunes in the late 1800s. Josephson pointed out that these men were becoming as powerful as *feudal* lords. However, feudal lords had protected their subjects. The robber barons

自由企业和政府监管之间的紧张关系

"强盗资本家"一词是由社会批评家马修·约瑟夫森首次使用的。它是指在19世纪末期创造了财富的一些富商们。约瑟夫森指出，这些人正变得和封建领主一样强大。然而，封建领主保护了他们的臣民。而强盗资本家们靠剥削工人变得富有，却完全不顾及他们

---

expression *n.* 表达   critic *n.* 批评家
feudal *adj.* 封建制度的

got rich by exploiting their workers without regard for the workers' welfare.

Many *historians* now credit these *tycoons* with making America a great industrial nation. They built the railroads that connected the East and West coasts. They provided the coal and other resources that powered factories. Their methods, however, were *ruthless*. They used their control of resources such as coal to keep prices high. Their large companies forced smaller ones out of business. Children as young as six worked all day in their mines and their factories.

These excesses made people see the need to set some limits on free enterprise. In 1887 Congress established a federal agency to control the railroads. That agency, the Interstate Commerce

的福利。

很多历史学家现在把使美国成为大工业国的功劳归功于这些企业界大亨。他们修建了连接东海岸和西海岸的铁路。他们提供了工厂动力的煤炭和其他资源。然而，他们的方法是无情的。他们利用对如煤炭等资源的控制来维持高价。他们的大公司使小公司被迫歇业。6岁的儿童要在矿山和工厂工作一整天。

这些过度的行为使人们看到有必要对自由企业设置一些限制。1887年，国会建立了一个联邦机构来控制铁路。被称为州际商务委员会的机

historian *n.* 历史学家 tycoon *n.* 巨头
ruthless *adj.* 无情的；残忍的

Commission, was the first that had the power to make rules for private businesses. Today, more than 100 *regulatory* agencies can make rules.

Many of these agencies were formed to protect the public. The *Occupational* Health and Safety Administration makes rules for safety on the job. The Food and Drug Administration decides which drugs are safe to use and protects the food supply.

Other agencies ensure fair *competition*. The Federal Trade Commission (FTC) keeps companies from agreeing to charge the same price for their goods. The FTC must also review and approve *mergers* that might give one company too much control of an industry.

构，是第一个有权力对私营企业制定规则的机构。今天，有100多个监管机构可以制定规则。

许多类似机构的设置是为了保护公众。职业健康和安全管理部门为工作安全制定规则。食物和药物管理部门决定哪种药物可以安全使用并确保粮食供应。

其他一些机构来确保公平竞争。联邦贸易委员会保持所有公司同意他们的货物以相同的价格销售。联邦贸易委员会还必须审查和批准可能带给一个公司在一个行业中过多控制权的并购行为。

---

regulatory *adj.* 管理的；控制的　　　　occupational *adj.* 职业的
competition *n.* 竞争　　　　　　　　　merger *n.* 合并

At first government agencies had only narrow powers. Then concern grew over problems that can affect more than one industry, such as pollution. After the Environmental Protection Agency was formed to watch for problems that affect the environment, other agencies with broad powers were set up in the 1980s. At the same time, some industries were "*deregulated*" (rules affecting airlines and *utilities* were eased).

Debate over *regulation* goes on. In 1999 it cost businesses more than $750 billion to follow federal guidelines. Some say that these rules are a great burden on the economy. Others say that the *collapse* of giant companies such as Enron and WorldCom shows the need for tighter rules.

起初政府机构的权利有限。后来政府开始关注可以影响多个行业的问题，如污染。在关注影响环境问题的环境保护署成立后，拥有广泛权力的其他机构在20世纪80年代也相继成立。与此同时，一些行业也被"撤销管制"（影响航空业和公用事业的规则被放松了）。

人们对管理的讨论还在进行。1999年企业花费7500多亿元来遵循联邦的指导方针。有些人认为，这些规则是对经济的巨大负担。其他人认为巨头公司，如安然公司和世通公司的崩溃显示，需要对企业制定更严格的规则。

---

deregulate *v.* 解除管制　　　　　　　　　　utility *n.* 公用事业
regulation *n.* 规章制度　　　　　　　　　　collapse *n.* 崩溃

37

Food from the 'Hood

In 1992, students at Crenshaw High School turned a garden into a business. Food from the 'Hood began as a response to violent Los Angeles riots. One cause of the riots was the *verdict* in the Rodney King trial, in which an all-white *jury acquitted* four police officers accused of beating an African American man. The

来自社区的食物

1992 年，克伦肖高中的学生们用花园做起了生意。"来自社区的食物"开始成为对洛杉矶暴动的回应。暴动的原因之一是对罗德尼·金一案的判决，在案件中一个全都由白人组成

---

verdict *n.* 判决
acquit *v.* 宣判无罪

jury *n.* 陪审团

students also saw another reason for the riots: lack of economic *opportunity*.

The students responded by forming their own natural-foods business. A teacher and a volunteer adviser helped them make a plan. In October, the student-owners planted crops in a garden behind the school. By late December, they had *donated* their first harvest to a neighborhood food bank.

The next year, they developed their quarter-acre garden into a business *asset*. They sold their produce at a local farmer's market. They also started a line of salad dressings. Half of the profits were used to expand their company. The rest went into a *scholarship* fund.

的陪审团，宣判被指控殴打一个美国黑人的四名警察无罪。学生们也看到了暴动的另一个原因：缺乏经济机会。

学生们的回应是通过建立他们自己的天然食品业务。一名教师和一名志愿者顾问帮助他们制定了一个计划。10月，学生们在学校后面的花园种植了作物。12月末，他们把他们第一次的收获捐赠给了临近的食物银行。

第二年，他们把四分之一英亩的花园开发成商业资产。他们在当地的农贸市场出售他们的农产品。他们也开始制作沙拉酱。一半的利润用来拓展他们的公司，其余的用来做奖学金基金。

---

opportunity *n.* 机会
asset *n.* 资产

donate *v.* 捐赠
scholarship *n.* 奖学金

Today students still learn business skills by managing Food from the 'Hood. They give one-quarter of their produce to *the needy*. Their products bring in $250 thousand a year.

As students expand the company, they also *cultivate* their futures. More than 70 students who were once at risk of dropping out have gone on to college.

如今，学生们仍然在通过管理"来自社区的食物"学习商业技能。他们把四分之一的产品给予有需要的人。他们的产品每年带来25万美元的收入。

学生们在拓展公司的同时，也在培养他们的未来。70多名曾经有辍学危险的学生都进入了大学。

---

the needy 穷人   cultivate *v.* 培养

38

The Emancipation Proclamation: "A Fit and Necessary War Measure"

In 1862 the Civil War was going badly for the North. President Abraham Lincoln knew that he must take action. The Emancipation Proclamation, issued on January 1, 1863, was his way of adding new meaning to the struggle. The document *declared* that all enslaved persons in states and *territories* in active *rebellion*

《解放黑人奴隶宣言》："一项恰当而必要的战争措施"

1862年内战战势对北方极其不利。林肯总统意识到他必须采取行动以扭转形势。发布于1863年1月1日的《解放黑人奴隶宣言》就是他用自己的方式对这场斗争所加入的新的意义。该文件宣布，从那天起反叛美国的各州及各地区的所有被奴役的人，

---

declare *v.* 宣布   territory *n.* 领域
rebellion *n.* 反叛

against the United States would from that day on be free.

In private life, Lincoln had always been against slavery. As president, however, his first *priorities* were to *uphold* the Constitution and preserve the Union. Before the South actively rebelled against the United States, Lincoln took a middle ground in his policy toward slavery. During his campaign, he promised to "take no actions as president to impair or limit slavery in those states where it existed." By 1861 all 11 Southern states had seceded from the Union. The Civil War had begun. From the start, the *foremost* aim of the North was to hold the United States together. Lincoln feared that the four border states, which were proslavery but also pro-Union, would join the Confederacy. Thus, he was careful to assume a neutral stance

都获得自由。

在他的一生中，林肯都在反对奴隶制。然而作为总统，他最先考虑的是支持宪法和保护国家。在南方发生激烈反叛之前，林肯在奴隶制方面采取的是中立政策。在竞选期间他承诺"不会对那些已经存在奴隶制的州采取措施去削弱或限制奴隶制"。到1861年所有南方的11个州都脱离了联邦政府，内战开始。起初北方的目的是保护国家的统一，林肯担心4个既支持奴隶州又支持政府的边界州会加入南方联盟。因此他谨慎地保持中立

---

priority *n.* 优先考虑的事　　　　　　　　　　　　　　uphold *v.* 支持
foremost *adj.* 首要的

on the issue.

As the war raged on, Lincoln saw that he could not *maintain* this *stance*. Union battle losses had piled up. The U.S. armed forces also were suffering *shortages* of men. Lincoln decided that freeing the enslaved people had finally become a "military necessity". Ironically, the Proclamation did not actually free anybody. Because the document applied only to the Confederate states, the United States could free people in the South only by means of victories. However, it turned the *tide* of the war. Enslaved people fled from their owners in the South and headed north. As a result, a valuable labor force shifted from the South to the North. The Emancipation Proclamation also opened the U.S. armed forces to African American recruits. About 200 thousand African Americans fought for the Union.

态度。

　　随着内战的进行，林肯发现不能再坚持这种立场。联邦政府战斗接连失利，同时美国的武装部队也缺乏士兵。林肯意识到释放奴隶最终成为了"军事需要"。讽刺的是宣言实际上没有让任何人获得自由。因为该文件只适用于南部联盟各州，美国要想使南方的人获得自由就必须取得战争的胜利。然而这就扭转了战争的局势。南方被奴役的人逃离了他们的主人，前往北方。结果，有价值的劳动力从南方流向北方。《解放黑人奴隶宣言》也为联邦政府军队补充了美国黑人士兵。大约20万美国黑人为联邦政

---

maintain *v.* 坚持；维持　　　　　　　　　　stance *n.* 态度；立场
shortage *n.* 缺少　　　　　　　　　　　　　tide *n.* 局势

Perhaps most important, the proclamation expanded the meaning of the Civil War. The war had become a battle not only to preserve the United States but also to end slavery. As a result, the South could no longer hope for the support of its chief trading partners, Great Britain and France. Both countries *opposed* slavery. The tide of battle shifted, and in April of 1865 the South *surrendered*. On December 18, 1865, the 13th Amendment to the Constitution outlawed slavery throughout the United States.

府而战。

　　也许最重要的是，该宣言扩大了内战的意义。这不仅仅是一次维护美国统一的战争，更是结束奴隶制的战争。结果，南方不能再寄希望得到他们主要贸易伙伴英国和法国的支持，因为这两国都反对奴隶制。战争的形势由此发生了转变，1865年4月，南方宣布投降。1865年12月18日，宪法第十三条修正案宣布奴隶制在全国不合法。

---

oppose *v.* 反对　　　　　　　　　　　　　　　　surrender *v.* 投降

39

The Fighting 54th

The Emancipation Proclamation *permitted* free African Americans and former enslaved people to join the U.S. armed forces. Several African American *regiments* were formed. Perhaps the most famous of these was the 54th Massachusetts Infantry. The troop consisted of about one thousand soldiers.

战斗的第五十四步兵团

《解放黑人奴隶宣言》允许获得自由的美国黑人和之前被奴役的人参军。一些美国黑人兵团成立，也许其中最出名的就是马萨诸塞州第五十四步兵团。这支部队大约有1000名士兵。宣言颁布后5个月，士兵们就做好了战斗准备。25岁的上尉罗伯特·萧被提拔

---

permit *v.* 允许   regiment *n.* 兵团

Five months after the Proclamation, the soldiers were ready to fight. Twenty-five-year-old Captain Robert Shaw was promoted to colonel. He *commanded* the 54th.

One of the regiment's first *assignments* was to burn and *loot* the small town of Darien, Georgia. Shaw *complained* that this was beneath the dignity of his men. He stressed the importance of African American troops' being actively engaged in battle. As a result, the regiment was ordered to South Carolina, where Union troops were fighting to capture the small islands that protected Charleston Harbor. On July 18, 1863, the 54th mounted an attack on heavily fortified Fort Wagner. Under heavy fire, Colonel Shaw led his

---

为陆军上校，由他来指挥第五十四兵团。

　　该兵团最初的任务之一就是焚烧和掠夺佐治亚州的达里恩小镇。萧抱怨这有违他士兵的尊严。他强调美国黑人部队积极参战的重要性。因此，该兵团被调往南卡罗来纳州，这里正为争夺保护查尔斯顿港湾的小岛屿而战斗。1863年7月18日，第五｜四兵团重创戒备森严的华格纳堡。在猛烈的攻击下，萧上校带领他的士兵们冲上了那倾斜的用沙袋加固的要塞城

---

command *v.* 指挥　　　　　　　　　　assignment *n.* 任务
loot *v.* 掠夺　　　　　　　　　　　　complain *v.* 抱怨

men up the sloped, *sandbagged* walls of the fort. Shaw was killed as he reached the top. In all, 281 members of the 54th died that day.

Although the attack was unsuccessful and Fort Wagner remained in Confederate control, the 54th gained *distinction* for its bravery and skill. A massive bronze *sculpture* on the Boston Common stands as a *memorial*. The film Glory tells the story.

墙。当他到达城墙上时被射杀了。那天第五十四兵团总共阵亡了281名士兵。

虽然那次袭击没有成功，华格纳堡仍然在南方联盟的控制下，但是第五十四兵团却因它的勇敢和战斗能力而赢得荣誉。大量的青铜雕塑耸立在波士顿公园作为纪念。影片《荣誉》讲述的就是这个故事。

sandbag *v.* 用沙袋加固   distinction *n.* 荣誉
scúlpture *n.* 雕像   memorial *n.* 纪念物

40

Jury Duty, Jury Rights

Most people think of jury service as a duty of *citizenship*. But it also can be viewed as a right. According to the U.S. Constitution, deciding guilt or *innocence* is not the only function of trial by jury. In a criminal trial, a jury also can refuse to apply a law. However, some people believe that *jurors* are taking this right too far.

陪审团的职责与权利

大多数人把任陪审员看做是公民的责任。但是它也可以被看做是一种权利。根据美国宪法，裁定有罪或者是无罪不是陪审团进行审判的唯一职能。在刑事审判中，陪审员也可以拒绝执行法律。然而，有些人认为陪审员的权利太过。

citizenship *n.* 公民   innocence *n.* 无罪
juror *n.* 陪审员

135

In a criminal trial, the state presents evidence of the *defendant's* guilt, and the defense tries to show that the defendant is not guilty. The jury weighs the evidence and comes to a verdict that must be *unanimous*—that is, all 12 jurors must agree. If even a single juror votes in opposition to the others, the case ends in a mistrial. For the state to get a *conviction*, it must retry the defendant.

A juror may have reasons for voting against the other jurors. The juror in question may honestly think that the evidence does not support a conviction. On the other hand, the juror may believe that the law itself is unjust or that it is being applied unfairly. The juror may believe that the defendant is not guilty according to those

---

在刑事审判中，政府提供被告人有罪的证据，辩护律师尽力证明被告人无罪。陪审团衡量证据，然后进行裁决，裁决必须是一致同意的——就是说，所有12个陪审员都必须同意。即使只有一个陪审员反对，这个案子也以未决审判结束。政府要给被告人定罪，必须进行再审。

陪审员可以有理由投票反对其他陪审员。提出质疑的陪审员可以公正地认为，证据不足不能定罪。另一方面，陪审员也可以认为法律本身是不公正的，或者被不公平地运用了。在这些情况下，陪审员可以认为被告

---

defendant *n.* 被告人
conviction *n.* 定罪

unanimous *adj.* 一致同意的

grounds. This practice, called jury *nullification*, can be traced back to colonial days. In 1735 newspaper publisher John Peter Zenger was tried for *libel* for printing *criticisms* of New York's governor. At the time, it was *illegal* to criticize the British king or his appointed officials publicly, but the jury acquitted Zenger.

The U.S. Supreme Court has upheld the right of jury nullification, and the practice has indeed been an important force in protesting unjust laws. The Zenger case, for example, established that published criticisms could not be considered libel if they were true. In this case, jury nullification reflected the values of the public. However, the practice becomes a problem when a single juror acts

---

是无罪的。这个制度就叫陪审团否决原则，它可以追溯到殖民地时期。1735年报纸出版商约翰·彼得·曾格因印刷批评纽约州长的评论而被以诽谤罪受审。那个时候，公开地评论英国国王或者他任命的官员都是不合法的，但是陪审团宣告曾格无罪。

美国最高法院支持了陪审团否决原则的权利，这个制度确实是抗议不公正法律的重要力量。比如，曾格的案子确立了这一点，如果发表的评论是真实的就不能认为是诽谤。在这个案子里，陪审团否决原则反映了民众的价值观。然而，当某个陪审员按强烈的个人偏见去行事，这个制度就是

---

nullification *n.* 否决原则   libel *n.* 诽谤
criticism *n.* 批评   illegal *adj.* 不合法的

on strong personal *bias*. Such a juror may nullify a jury in complete *disregard* of the law and the evidence, especially in *controversial* laws, such as those related to gun control.

The percentage of criminal cases ending in mistrial has steadily risen in recent decades. Some legal scholars believe that the legal system is put into peril when only one juror can cause a mistrial because of emotion or bias. Some legal scholars have suggested changing the law to make it no longer necessary for a verdict to be unanimous.

问题了。这样的陪审员可能不顾法律和证据否决陪审团，尤其是有争议的法律，比如，枪支管制的问题。

以未决审判结束的刑事案件的比例近几十年来稳定攀升。一些法律学者认为，当一个陪审员由于情感或偏见而引起未决审判时，法律系统就陷入了困境。一些法律学者建议修改法律，不再需要一致通过才进行裁决。

---

bias *n.* 偏见   disregard *n.* 无视
controversial *adj.* 有争议的

41

Selecting Judges

In a democracy, it is vital to have a court system in which judges are *independent*. They must be free to *interpret* the law without regard to public opinion or politics. Not everyone agrees, however, on the best way to achieve this goal.

State judges are appointed by the legislature or the *governor*. Under this

---

选举法官

在民主政治内，有法官独立的司法制度是至关重要的。他们必须自由地解释法律而不必考虑公众舆论和政治。然而，并非所有人都同意实现这个目标的最好方式。

州法官是由立法机关或者州长任命的。在这个制度下，官员可以任意

---

independent *adj.* 独立的
governor *n.* 州长

interpret *v.* 解释

system, officials are free to choose judges who are their *allies*, even though they may not be the best choices.

Allowing the public to elect its judges avoids this *pitfall*, but this system brings its own problems. It tends to turn judges into *politicians*. They become concerned with maintaining their *popularity*. This can affect their decisions in court. Also, conflicts may arise when they must decide cases involving their contributors. Finally, few voters are fully informed about the honesty or qualifications of candidates for judgeships, so there is no guarantee that the best judges will be elected.

Some people believe that merit selection is best. In this method, when an opening for a judgeship occurs, an independent

---

选择他们的同盟者做法官，即使他们可能不是最好的选择。

允许民众选举自己的法官可以避免这个隐患，但是这个系统也有它自己的问题。它倾向于把法官变成政客。他们会变得关心维护自己的声望。这可能会影响他们在法庭上的判决。另外，当他们裁决涉及他们捐助人的案件时，矛盾也许会升级。最后，几乎没有选民完全了解法官候选人的诚信或者资格，所以，没人能保证选出最好的法官。

有些人认为优选是最好的。在这个方式中，当有法官职位空缺时，独

---

ally *n.* 盟友
politician *n.* 政客

pitfall *n.* 隐患
popularity *n.* 声望

committee screens candidates. This body forwards to the governor or other official a list of those approved. Then that official makes an appointment from the list. Critics point out, however, that the committee itself is made up of *appointees*. As a result, *appointments* may not be truly unbiased.

立的委员会就会筛选候选人。这个委员会给州长或是其他官员提交一个获准人名单。然后官员从名单中任命法官。然而评论家们指出，委员会本身就是由被任命者组成的。因此，任命可能不是真正公正的。

---

appointee *n.* 被任命者   appointment *n.* 任命

42

The Haitian Revolution: Casting Out the Caste System

In the late 1780s, the French colony of Saint-Domingue was at the peak of its *prosperity*. It was the world's leading sugar producer. This Caribbean colony of some 560 thousand persons owed its success to the enslaved people who worked its *plantations*. The social system was a strict caste system. It used skin color to

海地革命：废除等级制度

在18世纪80年代末，圣多明克的法国殖民统治处于繁荣的顶峰。当时它是世界主要的甘蔗生产地。这个拥有560 000多人口的加勒比殖民区把成功归根于在其种植园工作的奴隶们。社会制度是一种严

---

prosperity *n.* 繁荣   plantation *n.* 种植园

determine one's place in society.

The people of Saint-Domingue were broadly separated into a white upper class and a black *underclass*. There were *distinctions* within these castes, however. At the top of the upper class were the *seigneurs*, or *lords*. These wealthy, white, slaveholding planters owned the plantations and wielded all the power. Under them were white officials, aligned with the government. They worked to keep the planters in power. Under them were poor whites, such as merchants and overseers, who performed duties for the planters. These poor whites had no real power or wealth, but they did have rights before the law. They considered themselves superior to the black underclass, even those much wealthier than they. At the time, the white upper class numbered about 32 thousand.

格的等级制度。因肤色来判断一个人的社会地位。

圣多明克的人民从广义上可分为以白人为主的上层阶级和以黑人为主的下层阶级。然而在这些阶级内部也有区别。上层阶级的顶端是封建领主或是君主。这些富裕的白人奴隶主拥有种植园并支配着所有的权力。在他们之下是和政府结盟的白人官员。他们的工作是维护种植园主的权力。再往下是贫穷的白人，比如商人和工头，他们的职责是为种植园主履行职责。这些穷困的白人没有实际权力或是财富，但是在法律面前他们却是有权利的。他们认为自己比黑人阶级高级，即使是那些比这部分白人还有钱的黑人。当时，白人上层阶级的人数大约是32 000人。

---

underclass *n.* 下层阶级
seigneur *n.* 领主

distinction *n.* 区别
lord *n.* 君主

At the top of the underclass were some 24 thousand free Africans (nonenslaved persons, including those who had been freed) and free people of mixed race. These freed Africans had no social equality with the white upper class but were *frequently* landholders of substance, owning one-third of the real *estate* and one-fourth of the wealth. Although they had no legal rights, they did share in the wealth. At the bottom of the caste system were *roughly* 500 thousand enslaved people, many newly arrived from Africa. They had no rights, no land, and no money. Without them, however, the colony would have *perished*.

After the slave rebellion of 1791, led by a former enslaved person named Toussaint Louverture, Saint-Domingue's racist caste system was transformed. By 1801 Louverture had maneuvered his way into

---

在下层阶级的顶端是24 000左右自由的非洲人（包括没有被奴役的黑人，还有那些已经获得自由的黑人）还有一些混合种族的自由人。这些自由的非洲人没有和白人上层阶级平等的社会地位，但却常常是有钱的地主，他们掌握着三分之一的房产和四分之一的财富。尽管他们没有合法权利，但是很有钱。在等级制度的最底层大约有50万受奴役的黑人，很多都是从非洲新来的。他们没有权利、土地和钱。然而没有他们，这个殖民地可能已经消失了。

1791年一个之前是奴隶的名叫杜桑·卢维杜尔的人发动奴隶起义后，圣多明克的种族等级制度就被转变了。到1801年，卢维杜尔通过自

---

frequently *adv.* 经常地
roughly *adv.* 大约；大致

estate *n.* 房产
perish *v.* 消失

ruling a largely self-governing state. His new constitution *abolished* slavery. It also *banned* racial discrimination in the civil service. However, his new society was not a democracy. Louverture was ruler for life.

In 1802 France tried to reestablish the slave state of Saint-Domingue, *overthrowing* Louverture in the process; but his second-in-command, the fierce Jean-Jacques Dessalines, foiled French plans. On January 1, 1804, Dessalines unveiled the new Republic of Haiti, from the name used by the Arawak, the original inhabitants of the island.

己的方式统治了一个庞大的自治政府。他的新宪法是废除了奴隶制，同时在行政部门内禁止种族歧视。但是他的新社会体制并不是民主制度，他是一个终身统治者。

在1802年法国尝试重新建立圣多明克的奴隶制政体，并在这过程中推翻了卢维杜尔。但是他的副手，愤怒的让·雅克·德萨林，击溃了法国的计划。在1804年1月1日，德萨林宣布了新的海地共和国成立，这个名字是由岛上原始居民阿拉瓦人使用的。

abolish *v.* 废除　　　　　　　　　　　　　　　　　　ban *v.* 禁止
overthrow *v.* 推翻

43

Toussaint Louverture, the Sudden Hero

Born in 1743 in Saint-Domingue, François Dominique Toussaint was the son of an educated slave. After he was legally freed in 1777, he *reared* a family and lived a simple life. Well into middle age, he *abruptly* met his destiny during the slave revolt of 1791.

Soon after helping his former master to

突然成为英雄的杜桑·卢维杜尔

杜桑1743年生于圣多明克，他是一个受过教育的奴隶的儿子。在1777年合法获得自由后，他养家糊口，过着简单的生活。他平稳地进入中年，在1791年奴隶起义期间他意外地改变了自己的命运。

在他帮助以前的主人成功逃脱后不久，杜桑加入了反叛军队。他很沮

---

rear *v.* 抚养   abruptly *adv.* 意外地；突然地

escape, Toussaint joined the revolt. He was *dismayed* to see how poorly organized the troops were. He began to *assemble* his own army, training and drilling the men in *guerrilla warfare*. Two years later, as a highly regarded general, Toussaint added Louverture to his name. This is French for overture or introductory section. The name may well have signaled a new direction in his life.

Louverture was endowed with great vigor and drive. He was a charismatic leader, inspiring love and loyalty. He was determined to end slavery and rule a self-governing country. Louverture outmaneuvered Britain, Spain, and particularly France to achieve this goal.

丧地发现军队的组织很差。他开始集结自己的军队，在游击战中培养和训练士兵。两年后，作为一名受重视的将军，杜桑把卢维杜尔加到自己的名字里。这个词是法语里的"序曲"或是"开场白"的意思。这个名字也很好地表明他人生中的新方向。

　　卢维杜尔天生具有很强的影响力和魄力。他是一名有魅力的领导者，鼓励仁爱和忠诚。他决定终结奴隶制并建立自治的国家。卢维杜尔运用策略击败了英国、西班牙，尤其是法国，从而实现了自己的目标。

---

dismay *v.* 沮丧　　　　　　　　　assemble *v.* 集结
guerrilla *n.* 游击队员　　　　　　warfare *n.* 战争

By 1801 Louverture controlled all of Hispaniola. The following year, the French *mounted* a huge armed campaign to take back Saint-Domingue, crushing Louverture's forces. Louverture gave up his power on the condition that slavery not be reestablished. His power gone, he was wrongly imprisoned by the French. He died in 1803, a year before the newly *renamed* Republic of Haiti won independence.

到1801年卢维杜尔控制了整个海地岛。第二年，法国加大火力在战争中夺回圣多明克，粉碎了卢维杜尔的武装势力。卢维杜尔在不恢复奴隶制的前提下放弃了自己的权力。他的政权消失了，被法国政府不正当地送进监狱。他死于1803年，一年之后重新命名的海地共和国取得独立。

mount *v.* 增加   rename *v.* 重命名

44

Jefferson and Hamilton: Hate that Shaped a Nation

As two of America's founders, Thomas Jefferson and Alexander Hamilton shared many goals and ideals, yet they strongly disliked one another. This dislike arose from their *opposing* backgrounds, values, and visions for their new country. Strangely, the more *hostile* their clashes grew, the more creative a

杰弗逊和汉密尔顿：仇恨塑造了一个国家

作为美国的两大开国元勋，托马斯·杰弗逊和亚历山大·汉密尔顿有着共同的目标和理念，但是他们却极其讨厌对方。这种讨厌源于他们对立的背景、价值观，以及对于新国家的看法。奇怪的是，他们敌对的冲突越多，他们就越具有创造力。这两位伟人的论战形成了今天

---

opposing *adj.* 相反的；对立的　　　　　　　　　hostile *adj.* 敌对的

force they became. The battles waged between these two brilliant men helped define the ideas and *institutions* that shape American life, law, and politics to this day.

Hamilton was a man of humble birth. His father had abandoned the family when he was a boy. Jefferson was born into a *landowning* family with powerful *connections*. It was Hamilton, not Jefferson, however, who believed that the country would be best led by a strong central government made up of wealthy *aristocrats*. He believed that presidents and senators should be elected for life. Jefferson was a passionate advocate for equality. He held that people of all stations should have a say in government. His ideal was a country founded on the needs and virtues of people who lived

---

美国生活、法律和政治的思想和制度。

汉密尔顿出身平民。当他还是个孩子时，他的父亲就抛弃了家庭。而杰弗逊则是出生在一个拥有权力的地主家庭。然而恰恰是汉密尔顿，而不是杰弗逊，认为一个国家最好应该由富有的贵族组成强大的中央政府去领导。他认为总统和参议员应该被选举成终身任职。杰弗逊则是拥护平等的人。他认为所有阶层的人都应有在政府中的发言权。他理想的国家是建立

---

institution *n.* 制度　　　　　　landowning *adj.* 拥有土地的
connection *n.* 关系　　　　　　aristocrat *n.* 贵族

close to the land. He promoted a small central government. These principles became known as Jeffersonian democracy.

Trouble first brewed when both men served in President George Washington's *cabinet*. Although the Revolutionary War had ended, Great Britain still held some forts in the Northwest Territories. Jefferson, as *secretary of state*, wanted to use trade sanctions to force the British out. Hamilton, as secretary of the *treasury*, did not want to risk losing revenue. His position won out, and no trade *restrictions* were imposed.

The men's differences reached a peak over Hamilton's proposal to set up a national bank. Hamilton supported business interests. He believed that such a bank would help the government regulate its

---

在人们的需要和道德上。他主张建立一个小型的中央政府。这些原则被称为杰弗逊民主主义。

当两人共同从政于乔治·华盛顿总统的内阁时，矛盾就已悄然滋生。尽管独立革命已经结束，但是英国仍然在西北领土占据一些要塞。作为国务卿的杰弗逊想使用贸易制裁来迫使英国出境，但是作为财政部部长的汉密尔顿并不想冒失去国民收入的风险。汉密尔顿的观点被采纳了，美国政府没有实行贸易限制。

俩人的分歧真正达到巅峰是在汉密尔顿提出建立国民银行时。汉密尔

---

cabinet *n.* 内阁
treasury *n.* 财政部

secretary of state 国务卿
restriction *n.* 限制

finances. Jefferson was wary of such a plan. He feared that it would give the government too much power, encourage *irresponsible* use of the nation's money supply, and hurt farmers.

This debate came to include the broader question of the power of the U.S. Constitution. Jefferson pointed out that the Constitution did not expressly permit the formation of a national bank. *Therefore*, such a bank would be *unconstitutional*. Hamilton responded that any powers not prohibited by the Constitution would automatically be allowed. This line of reasoning became known as the implied-powers *doctrine*. Again, Hamilton's views prevailed over Jefferson's. The implied-powers doctrine was upheld by the U.S. Supreme Court and continues to guide lawmaking today.

顿支持商业利益，并且认为这个中央银行将会对政府管理财政起到帮助。杰弗逊对于这个计划持怀疑的态度，他担心这将会赋予政府太多的权力，促使政府对国家的货币供应不负责任，损害农民的利益。

这场争论甚至还涉及美国宪法的权力范围。杰弗逊指出宪法并没有明确表示允许建立国民银行，因此这是违反宪法的。而汉密尔顿则回应道，宪法没有禁止的任何权力都应该自动生效。关于宪法界定的理论后来被称之为"暗含权力论"。再一次，汉密尔顿的观点占了上风。美国最高法院认可了汉密尔顿所提出的观点，并且这一观点依然在指导着美国今天的立法。

---

irresponsible *adj.* 不负责任的

unconstitutional *adj.* 违反宪法的

therefore *adv.* 因此

doctrine *n.* 主义；学说